ID0984278

MADAGASCAR TRAVELS

MADAGASCAR TRAVELS

Christina Dodwell

Hodder & Stoughton

British Library Cataloguing in Publication Data

Dodwell, Christina
Madagascar Travels
I. Title
916.91045

ISBN 0-340-62563-5

Typeset by Phoenix Typesetting, Ilkley, West Yorkshire
Printed and bound in Great Britain by Mackays of Chatham PLC

Hodder and Stoughton
a division of Hodder Headline PLC
338 Euston Road
London NW1 3BH

CONTENTS

ILLUSTRATIONS

All photographs by the author

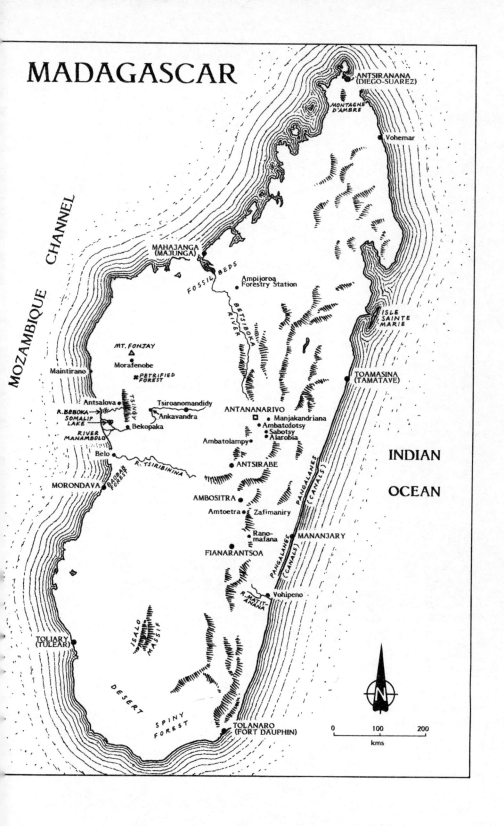

MADAGASCAR

ANTSIRANANA
(DIEGO-SUAREZ)

MONTAGNE
D'AMBRE

Vohemar

MAHAJANGA
(MAJUNGA)

FOSSIL BEDS

Ampijoroa
Forestry Station

ISLE
SAINTE
MARIE

MT. FONJAY
Morafenobe

Maintirano

PETRIFIED
FOREST

TOAMASINA
(TAMATAVE)

Antsalova
TSINGY
Tsiroanomandidy

R. BEBOKA
SOMALIP
LAKE
Ankavandra

ANTANANARIVO
Manjakandriana

Bekopaka
Ambatofotsy
Sabotsy
Alarobia

RIVER
MANAMBOLO

Belo
Ambatolampy

R. TSIRIBIHINA
ANTSIRABE

INDIAN

OCEAN

MORONDAVA
BAOBAB
FOREST

AMBOSITRA

Amtoetra Zafimaniry

Ranomafana

MANANJARY

FIANARANTSOA

PANGALANES (CANALS)

Vohipeno

R. MATIT-
ANANA

PANGALANES (CANALS)

ISALO
MASSIF

TOLIARY
(TULEAR)

DESERT

SPINY
FOREST

TOLANARO
(FORT DAUPHIN)

0   100   200
kms

N

MOZAMBIQUE CHANNEL

BETSIBOKA RIVER

ONE

By Stagecoach Through a Cyclone

1

IT WAS DARK inside the stable and I had to squeeze past the rumps of a couple of horses to look at the two furthest bay stallions. I paused at a fat mare, but fat females would probably be pregnant, so I chose two sleek compact males and checked their coats for sores.

The wooden stagecoach they would pull was outside the stable, yellow-painted with red around its windows, a green base and blue roof. Locally called a calèche, it was normally used to bring people and fresh vegetables into market. We agreed a price for me to hire the team for a week. Edouard, the proprietor of the horses and stagecoach, would come as main driver and teach me to drive, to which I looked forward. We would meet three days later, giving him time to drive east into the rural area of Manjakandriana where my journey would begin.

The capital's province of Antananarivo (Tana) has always intrigued me. Every time I fly to Madagascar the plane comes in over its high plateau rustic village life. But it is usually ignored by people who tend either to stay in Tana or to travel directly off to Madagascar's far-flung ends.

So on the Monday I found the stagecoach and crew, as planned, and piled my baskets and baggage on the roof-rack, tying it firmly in place alongside sacks of grass and crushed manioc for the horses' lunch. I noticed we had sensibly brought a spare wheel, the wheels being wooden spoked with strips of old truck tyre nailed around the rim. In through the coach's small half-door we stashed the food supplies, cookpots, and camping gear.

The driving seat was a raised lip on the front of the platform which jutted forward of the stagecoach body, and just behind it was a low bench with a cushion of rice-straw, where I decided to sit. One good thing about horse transport is that it doesn't use petrol and there was currently a petrol crisis in Madagascar.

With a twirl of the whip the horses moved forward, trotting, eager for new ground. Edouard said they had never been this far from the city before. Since it was market day in Manjakandriana we shopped for last-minute items and I bought a straw hat with broad enough brim to double as an umbrella. I didn't need to be too involved in food supplies for the week, having appointed a local man, Roland, to be guide, quartermaster, and translator. There were also two lads whose job was to cook and look after the horses.

Soon we had left the town behind and were rattling along a broad valley of rice paddies. The kaleidoscope of greens and yellows showed different stages of maturity from emerald and unripe to golden and mature. On the narrow dykes people were walking with baskets balanced on their heads. Threshing of rice was in process at points by the road, both men and women taking turns to beat sheaves against convenient boulders.

The Merina people of the central plateau mostly have straight black hair, mid- or light-brown skin, with dark eyes and high cheek-bones; they are slim-built and not very tall, all indications of their origins in Malaysia or Indonesia, whence they came in successive waves, probably via East Africa, during the first five centuries AD. On the coasts the people are often quite tall and much darker with curly or even woolly hair, showing their descent from later immigrants from Africa. It seems that only 2,000 years ago this huge island had no human inhabitants. There are myths about a pygmy aboriginal race occupying the centre of the island when the first Indonesians arrived, but no evidence to support them.

Around us people scurried about making fan-shapes of win-nowed straw and sweeping up stray grains of rice, originally brought to Madagascar by the Malay-Indonesian migrants whose diet and cultural lifestyle depended on it. The Malagasy calen-dar is based on its cycle of preparation, growth and harvest, and it is used as a measure of weight (the kapok-tinful) and of time – the time it takes a pot of rice to cook, the time it takes for seedlings to sprout.

The road was of hard-baked laterite and the horses clipped along at a trot. Edouard said he had brought his blacksmith's tools and spare horseshoes, and the only other preparations he had made for the journey were to grease the axles and sweep clean the interior.

Then he showed me how to use the reins. The two right reins joined over the right-hand horse's withers and came into the right hand. The left worked the same way to the left in a simple but efficient cat's cradle. The reins were made from jute which is the softened bark of a palm tree. The rest of their harness, the collars and traces attaching each horse to the crossbar under our feet, was made from a few bits of leather stitched and pinned with cord and wire to strips of tyre rubber and bits of cloth. The horses were not between shafts, they were harnessed to a single pole two and a half metres long. The go-faster noises were *ay-yeh*, *ghee* and *hya*, the aspirant grunts of *argh* and *haih*.

We crossed a rickety plank bridge and overtook a couple of zebu-carts. When we met one of these humpbacked oxen coming towards us with a load of wood, it suddenly swerved into our path but their driver averted a collision by jumping down to pull his beasts aside as we bounded past.

At roadside stalls piles of bananas and keki fruit, and plastic jerrycans of *toaka gasy*, illegal home-made rum, were displayed for sale. The occasional tall-gabled houses were two storeys high, and made of locally baked red mud-brick, the more ambitious plastered outside and coloured with dark brick corners and pink inset walls or other earthy-toned combinations.

Verandahs and balconies, held up by brick pillars, spilled roses, vines and orchids. The windows had wooden shutters, and the roofs were straw-thatched or tiled with scallop shaped clay tiles, sporting carved wood spikes on top of their gable ends. Some were three-storey with top windows gabled on to the steep roofslope. I guessed that was the kitchen because women's heads often popped out of those windows to have a look as we passed.

Dogs rushed up barking and children ran alongside laughing with excitement at the horses. Ahead of us a goose was running for its life. In a flooded area people in rice paddies worked thigh-deep in water, scything rice and pulling the floating bundles behind them through the waterlilies that covered any open water. So much water meant an increasingly muddy road with invisible potholes. Horse No. 1 stepped in a pothole up to his knees. He stumbled heavily but didn't fall, the momentum of the carriage helping him keep his balance.

The valley steepened and its sides were terraced for manioc, maize and spinach. There were banks of cosmos in purple, mauve and white flower. Where the road came hard up against the valley slope there was a landslide of red mud and fallen trees, recent, but cleared back enough for us to pass. It was one of many caused by last month's cyclone Geralda (the worst for nearly seventy years), which also damaged some of the bridges. We had some minor troubles with a couple of partially collapsed culverts but the first big bridge we crossed was all right. According to Roland another cyclone with hurricane force winds was being forecast. They were normal at this time of year.

Low branches of wattle trees scraped the roof. We ambled on through a village with an empty-looking primary school and a grocery called 'Epicerie Espérance'. From its recent colonial past French is the second language still in Madagascar and what I hoped to manage with. The road forked and we went south. It was as well Roland knew the way as there were no roadsigns; he had grown up in this region, an easy-going countryman, unpolished and good-natured. As they started getting to know each other the men talked in musical voices with long urrrs between words.

At noon we planned to stop at the village of a locally famous *ombiasy* or traditional healer and sorcerer. Traditional medicine has long been respected in Madagascar; the rainforests are full of medicinal plants and the knowledge of their use has been passed through the generations. Western medicine is hard to obtain and so expensive the ordinary people cannot afford it, Roland said, and anyway they prefer their own ancestral remedies. These start from the basis that illness, accident or misfortune may have more than a physical cause. You don't cure the illness, you cure the individual person. After diagnosis the treatment may be herbal, or consist of carrying out certain actions, such as a sacrifice, but these were usually ineffective without the healer's invocations or charms.

As we wound upwards into some hills, sun and fine rain made a misty spray. Tea and bananas were growing together in a landscape of granite domes and rounded boulders. Roland pointed out a bush similar to tea from which you can make a tisane to drink or put in your bath, and, like lavender essence it refreshes your skin and your mind. He said it's especially good when you're tired.

Traffic was still very scarce, only some zebu-carts laden with rice going back to be threshed in the villages. Occasionally there was a small drama when zebu panicked at the sight of horses. At one meeting as we inched past, everyone muttering *mora-mora* (take it easy), the zebu turned sharply and tried to bolt. Their yoke hit our horses and tangled with the reins. There was a churning of beasts. One zebu broke his harness and fled into the bush. The other was bucking around still attached to the cart, about to overturn it. Our horses were remarkably calm during the whole episode. The left-hand one was the better animal, the one on the right was tetchy, trying to bite his partner whenever the reins asked him to slow up.

The river was now to our left with many cascades where it dropped in foaming torrents among large boulders and passed beneath a long concrete bridge.

Tombs dotted across the hills were the main feature of the countryside, big square and rectangular tombs made of undressed stone, about two metres tall. The doors were massive stone slabs, partially buried, one had incised patterns on the lintel, and some were topped with fancy stonework. Roland explained that they extended underground and there would be a chamber with twenty to thirty corpses stacked on a bunk shelving system, wrapped simply in cloth or silk shrouds. Direct families (called *demes*) are kept together, but there can be several *demes* per tomb. He told me people want their tombs to be more permanent than their houses. There's a saying, 'A house is for a lifetime; a tomb is for eternity.' In Madagascar people probably spend more money on death and death-related celebrations than they do on living, as if life is only a preparation to becoming a great ancestor. 'We are part of a continuation, the family,' said Roland, 'and at ceremonies at the family tomb it is compulsory for the whole family to be there, you can't say you have anything more important to do.'

Everything depends on the ancestors, the health and prosperity of your family are controlled by them. Without their blessing, nothing can work well. Dead ancestors are potent forces that play an active part in daily life.

The most common tomb ceremony is *famadihana* or 'turning the bones', when the tomb doors are opened and the corpses are carried out of the tomb for rewrapping. The assembled family greet the dead, dance with them, sing to them, tell them the family gossip, and let them know they are not forgotten. Musicians called *hira gasy* are brought to entertain them, and finally the ancestors are rewrapped in a new silk *lamba* and stacked back in the tomb. *Lambas* are the all-purpose garments of Madagascar, worn sometimes as a sarong by men and women. How they are draped shows whether women are single, married or widowed. Silk *lambas* are for best and of course the ancestors deserve nothing but the best.

The custom of second burial is a distinctive feature in parts of Madagascar. Roland explained how types of tombs and burial rituals vary among the island's eighteen tribes, from the Merina mausoleums to Bara cave-tombs or Mahafaly carved funerary totems. All have an ancestor cult, and some disturb the dead while others leave them in peace.

Positioning your tombs in relation to the village has strictly observed rules. It is forbidden to build them to the east of houses, which is the place of worship and sacrifice, and sunrise, a powerful time of day. The north is also banned because it is the sunny and happy direction, while sorrow belongs on the cold south side of a village. North-east, south-east or south-west are appropriate for tombs, but their shadow must not touch the homes of the living. If it is impossible to comply with these rules, a special charm can be buried in the shadow to remove its danger. Other prohibited sites for a tomb are at the mouth of a valley because by dominating the valley it would draw the living into it; nor should it be built on poor land or 'hungry soil' because it would be searching for people to consume. The tomb's desire to consume is a particularly strong belief to the south. No tomb may be sited above the family home or the living will be weighed down with constant pressure and worry caused by the spirits of the dead; and though the doors of the living and the dead must both face west, care is taken to ensure the house of the dead is built at an angle to the house of the living to prevent them sharing the same *vintana* or destiny.

The next culvert was partly washed away and we manoeuvred on to it via a strip of earth supported by logs with long narrow gaps between them, lethal for horses and thin wheels. Edouard looked serious, the horses must avoid treading in the holes but if we squeezed hard left we should succeed in crossing. We edged past, all holding our breath, the only sound the creaking of the calèche as we moved across. Reaching the far side, we all decided it had been quite easy; none of us knew the capabilities of our stagecoach yet, nor of each other, but the other four assured me they were game for adventure and willing to face anything.

And so we arrived at the famous sorcerer's village, stopping just outside to unhitch the horses at a clearing where a stream ran across the road. Leaving the lads to sort out their needs, Roland took me to meet the *ombiasy*, Rahebita.

We went up the steep staircase into the modest room he used for consultations. By the dim light of a small window, I noticed a clutter of dried plants and cobwebs, and we brushed the dust off some stools to sit down. Rahebita was naturally very surprised by my visit, but being a long-standing friend of Roland, he was a gracious host and agreed to answer my questions. Over the next hour he explained that healing is a function of destiny. A particular day can make it unsuitable or ineffective for a particular cure. And apart from the nature of each day's destiny, each individual is born with a *vintana* linked, as with western astrology, to his birth moment. In Madagascar a person's destiny changes as he advances through time, moving into preordained good and bad periods, but people can use preventative measures to sidestep trouble and remove a *vintana*'s evil aspect. Preventing accident or illness is easier then curing it. You can be ill if you oppose your destiny. It is not a fatalistic approach, there are many opportunities to avoid problems. Calculating the interaction of personal *vintana* and astrological time is part of the *ombiasy*'s job.

Roland was gamely trying to translate into French but the *ombiasy* didn't stop talking with energy and enthusiasm. He said he learned his job from his father and grandfather, both healers, and that from early childhood he had been able to heal; he had always known he had the gift and was a member of the Guérisseurs Malagaches, the register of recognised island healers.

The other part of his astrological work is choosing days for events; for sowing or harvesting, marriages or entombments. It is important to work out the day with the best *vintana* for starting any enterprise, and different undertakings are advisable on different days, following the twelve-month lunar calendar, where each day and month's characteristic good or bad *vintana* alters with the changing phase of the moon.

Today was Monday which can bring sorrow and conflict, a good day for purification ceremonies; while Tuesday is a light and loose day, 'pierced through' and unreliable; a bad day for making important agreements or starting something permanent like building a home, it brings unfaithfulness and break-ups. But it is good for travel, idle stimulation, frivolity, and good for tilling the fields since its pierced aspect lets earth crumble easily. Wednesday is believed to 'bring no return', if you plant seed that day it will not bring much harvest, and if travelling, you risk not coming back. This makes it a good day for entombments, since the spirit will depart easily. This month, March, would see the end of the Malagasy year; then would come the first month, heralded by the biggest festival of the calendar, Alahamady, at the next new moon.

When we rejoined the stagecoach the lads had got a fire started and were thinking of cooking rice. Rahebita who we had invited to lunch suggested we go for a walk while they got on with it and he would show me the nearby sacred lake.

We walked uphill through pine and eucalyptus woodlands, glad for the shade since the midday sun was hot. The trees were planted by early colonials and are coppiced to provide charcoal and house-building poles. On the hilltop we came to a wrecked marketplace of red-earth brick and thatch. Rahebita explained it was smashed by fierce winds during Cyclone Geralda but had been a major regional market for cattle, chickens and cotton or silk *lamba*.

On a neighbouring hill we could see a village which Rahebita said was the home of former vassal-king Andrianatody and the birthplace of Queen Ranavalona III, the third wife of a nineteenth-century Prime Minister who married three queens in a row, a somewhat extreme way of staying in power. A standing stone at the back of the marketplace marked the spot where the nobles of the king divided the land into regions so it could be more easily ruled. The central plateau which forms the long spine of the island had been a patchwork of kingdoms ruled by petty monarchs who rose and fell in local wars, until the late 1700s when a powerful Merina king conquered and united them into a society with a recognised class system. Royalty and nobles were the Andriana; Roland and *ombiasy* Rahebita would be the middle caste of freemen, Hova; and the lowest were the serfs or Andevo. Cross-caste marriage was forbidden, though the Hova Prime Minister who collected queens seems to have managed to be upwardly mobile enough to bend the rules. The name of the king, which I made Roland repeat twice, was Andrianampoinimerinandriantsimitoviaminandriampanjaka. His son Radama I was an equally strong king who successfully united most of Madagascar.

We came over a rise and down to where the sacred lake Andrianandriana lay scooped between two valley arms. On the lakeshore a couple of fishermen were angling for tilapia which grow to two kilos because only certain people inherit the right to fish here. Kingfishers and butterflies flitted across the water.

In the time of the kings when there was a death in the royal family, the body and head would have gone into the royal family tomb, but the heart, intestines, stomach and lungs were sealed in a pottery urn, weighted and sunk in the middle of the lake where there were no currents to disturb it. Rahebita said the bottom has big stones and a fair number of urns still sitting among them.

He added that there is a *fady* (taboo) against swimming in the lake and at least twelve people are known to have drowned in it. Their deaths were inexplicable, but everyone knew they were caused by breaking the *fady*. Royal descendents are allowed to swim there. 'And others can try it,' he said, 'at their own risk.'

Before returning to the stagecoach we visited Rahebita's bee hives. There were fifteen of them, made of bits of hollow tree trunk and broken pottery urns, and yielding fifteen to twenty kilos of honey every couple of months. Honey is used in remedies and sacrifices. As an offering, it pleases the dead and keeps them quietly in their tombs. To make the bees leave the hive he calls them out using balm of citronelle smeared over a box. The bees adore the taste and get busy licking it while he deals with removing the honey. They normally feed on eucalyptus and wild flowers. I asked Rahebita if he ever got stung and he admitted he had once been quite badly attacked by his bees but, of course, he explained, he had the right plants to hand to remedy the stings.

Lunch of zebu meat and rice was ready when we returned. There was an amusing moment when we all waited for someone to unpack the plates and spoons. I looked at Roland, since he was quartermaster, and he looked at me as boss of the crew. Then each one of us sheepishly brought out our own personal bowl and utensils, which luckily we'd all brought, and my saucepan lid became Rahebita's bowl. Roland gave his second helping to an old man who came along and sat at the fire. I was pleased that I had insisted on not bringing the type of food that *vazaha* (foreigners) eat; it would be absurd to eat differently from the lads and anyway how can you understand the life of people if you don't eat the same food. And best of all, with Roland holding the purse to buy food, he bought the things the lads liked eating, so there were no complaints.

Bunches of children coming home from school stopped to look at the horses. They said they hadn't seen horses before. One group were counting the number of nails in the calèche. They found twenty-four. Others stood in awestruck groups around the horses and pushed small siblings to the front for a better view. You have to accept being part of an impromptu look and learn lesson when you are a *vazaha*.

2

When last I sat wondering where my travels might take me next, it suddenly struck me as blindingly obvious that I should tackle Madagascar. Having visited the island about six times over the past seven years, and kept a file on things I heard about there, I was surprised I hadn't realised sooner. Perhaps it was because it 'belonged' to other people, to the conservationists and wildlife experts, to those who had known the place far longer than I, to the eminent historian and former Ambassador to Madagascar, Sir Mervyn Brown, and to my husband who has visited Madagascar for Lloyds insurance work almost annually for twenty years. They all fell in love with it, it was their territory, and I felt I would be judged if I failed to appreciate the things they did.

Travel or exploration to me means going where others don't go. It is not necessary to go looking for uncontacted tribes, though I've done plenty of that in the past, it is simply a question of watching what others do then doing something different. In Madagascar this is made easier by the fact that the country lacks the infrastructure of Kenya-style tourism and the few visitors tend to follow the main roads. Getting around the island on these is not entirely hazard-free, but getting off the beaten track is easily begun. All you need to do is pick a poor road, follow it and hold your nerve. From the high plateau which has long been the heartland of Malagasy civilisation, I planned to range across the island. My main goals would be the eastern rain forest, the south-east coast with its mysterious Arab settlers, and the empty west where stone forests of pinnacles are reputed to hide remnants of the island's original inhabitants.

We only had nine kilometres to cover in the afternoon. We rumbled into motion and many of the children ran along behind. I watched how well Edouard handled his horses, always patient, flicking his whip in slow circles above his head but never touching the horses' backs. His face was thoughtful with wide-set eyes, tiny beard, and a strong jaw. He was just a few months older than me, in fact we were probably all much the same age. He said his liking for horses began because his father kept some, but young Edouard grew over six feet and too tall to ride any more. So he became a calèchier. Malagasy horses are small and wiry, shrinking smaller with successive generations of poor pasture and non-selective breeding. It struck me their evolution was in reverse and it needed some interference from abroad to improve the stock.

I was particularly interested in Malagasy horses because I wanted to find one to ride in a national horse race. This strange compulsion to become an amateur jockey is one of those things that comes upon me every ten years or so, and I had a sneaking suspicion that if I didn't do it now I might never screw myself up to it again. The only snag was I had to find a horse, and the horse-racing business in Madagascar did seem to be in some sort of terminal decline. It would be touch and go if I got round the local race course before it was condemned and pulled down.

I was jolted out of this melancholy reflection by Edouard swerving the horses to miss a chameleon walking across the track. It was the second I had seen that day. The earlier one had been sitting on a branch as I walked past and I had offered it a grasshopper. The chameleon's tongue shot out like elastic, as long as the creature's body, to seize its victim and whip it back into its mouth. The way a chameleon walks is strange with its shuddering ponderous gait, let alone the way the eyes swivel independently. It can look forwards and backwards at the same time. The Malagasy say it has one eye on the past and one on the future.

We rolled backwards at a gulley but made it across at the second attempt, then navigated through a troop of zebu and trotted on to lose a bunch of schoolkids. At a steep uphill stretch the lads jumped out to lighten the load. We had begun working as a team; the horses were pulling well, even the surly one had pricked up his ears and was clearly enjoying himself. Over the crest and along a contour, we could see basins of glittering water in emerald rice paddies and white and red earth houses, becoming fewer as the land grew emptier, with far views of forest which lay ahead for the morrow.

We jolted pleasantly along, got a bit lost at a crossroads, but Roland found the right way from a family at a further fork. A stony gulley made the horses stop dead, '*Gee, yuh,*' grunted Edouard and across we trundled. The jolting was noticeably hard, the leaf springs were worn out and we had no shock absorbers. But we felt we were equal to any problem.

Our destination for the night was the village of Ambohitrandri-amanitra on top of a hill to our south. The road was quite good until it forked again and we took the upper track, so deeply eroded with rain gulleys across it I wondered if it was really the main village connection. The horses hauled nicely up the first steep bit, then, turning a corner, we saw a very long hill ahead. The horses saw it too and refused to pull properly. They simply weren't trying and we ground to a halt. When they realised we were serious, they began to pull, scrabbling for a foothold. Horse 1 fell to its knees then was dragged upright again by the efforts of No. 2. We achieved a massive pull up the early part, then the gradient steepened again and we stopped to work out a strategy. As I was the lightest, Edouard said I should drive, while he encouraged the horses from the ground and the others pushed the stagecoach from behind.

So I took the reins and whip, whirling it round my head, and we clawed our way forward. A nasty backslide began where two gulleys met, the horses' feet could get no grip on the hard laterite, and we slid backwards at an alarming speed. I leapt forward on top of the pole shouting '*Hee, hoo,*' which goaded them into struggling to a halt, and the lads quickly pushed rocks under the back wheels to stop them rolling further.

We paused there to regain our breath, both beasts and men were puffing, and when Edouard checked the road ahead he said it was just as steep and without visible end. His normally calm face was tense. But he wasted no time complaining. He resigned himself to getting on with the job, even though it was more serious than anything he had imagined. Turning around now would be a highly dangerous manoeuvre, and we kept telling each other we could not be that far from the top, so we persevered up the mountain. The village had not looked inaccessible on the map and Roland said it was a particularly pretty one with glorious views from its hilltop. With much whooping and whip twirling we were moving grindingly slowly, another fifty metres, with profuse sweating from men and horses whose nostrils were flecked with foam.

We paused for another of many breathers, and attached a front rope to pull by. We knew the only way to get there was if each one did his best and it was a curiously bonding experience to work so hard together.

At the hilltop entering Ambohitrandriamanitra people lined the road to watch. I said stop watching and help push, and many came to help with a loud cheering. It was great to reach the top and we found the village clustered scenically on the summit with panoramic views to every side. The village name means 'village of the gods'.

The lane squeezed between tall, narrow houses, some with decoratively carved wooden balconies. Our entrance was spoiled by the calèche getting stuck in a narrow alley where we could not turn or back. So we unhitched the horses and Roland and I led them through some back lanes to an open plot hedged by vines where they could be tethered for the night. The task of manoeuvring the stagecoach out backwards was made more tricksy by the pole shaft swinging wildly as the front wheels veered in ruts. We leapt clear when it whammed past. The coach rocketed down a slope and the whole crowd of spectators jumped for their lives as the wheels spun and it careered backwards into a bank. Finally we rocked it safely into the shelter of a house.

Our first port of call was to meet the grandly titled President of the Fokontany, in effect the village headman. I was received courteously and the details of my identity were written into an old cloth-covered notebook by an elder so raggedly dressed his shirt had patched patches with yet more holes. We were given the use of an empty ground-floor room at the vice-president's house. Clean floor mats were laid out but no one took off their shoes since few people wore shoes anyway, and a crowd of people pressed inside to see what might be happening.

At dusk we lit two of our candles and put them either side of the window so I could see to write my diary; the window space quickly filled with a sea of faces, framed in candlelight. Inside was also jam-packed with people and to divert them I brought out my family photos and British postcards. Thank goodness for the photos. They cover the transition from being a stranger to being a person like anyone else. I gave them five minutes of discussing the photos, then shooed the crowd out, but the space was immediately filled by others. This time I explained the photos to the children. The queen and our royal family went down better than the scenes of town life. The children passed 'Roi Elizabeth' around with definite interest. Their last royal was King Andrianitoponimoronkay, dead for over a hundred years, without any living family. Before settling for the night I was allowed to look at two tombs on the hill summit in the centre of the village, but refused permission to visit the royal tomb because I was a stranger and did not yet understand the *fady*. I appreciated that they did not hold their sacred things lightly; if they had shown the tomb to me, it would cheapen it. If I had been staying for a few days, they explained, they could have allowed the visit.

So that I should not feel lonely, the whole of my host's family spent the evening with me. The women had massive numbers of children. They said that family sizes range between five and fifteen children, it being quite normal to have eight or ten. The vice-president's wife said that fourteen is the lucky number, and what one wished for at the time of marriage. Her last baby was born at dawn which meant he would be a good labourer and not lazy. Those born at midday may rise like the sun in honour and prestige, those born when the afternoon sun's rays slant through the door should enjoy golden riches flowing into their home, but if the birth is slow and the sun is setting, their life or property will become scattered and fade away.

Later in the evening we swopped songs; I sang them one of mine and persuaded them to sing me one of their harmony songs which split into many descants. The added attraction was that by recording it on my taperecorder we could all hear the playback. They understood the purpose of the magic box, but the delight at hearing their own voices for the first time was evident in their broad smiles and giggles.

When it came to time for us to go to sleep I unrolled my sleeping bag; we would sleep in a line. The men said I couldn't lie with my head to the south since only witches do that. Nor could we sleep with feet pointing east in case our feet kicked the sunrise. North was a draughty doorway so we all put heads to the east. Men usually sleep with their heads towards the north, their wives and children sleep with heads to the east. Three male snorers made the night wakeful and I lay hoping there would be a different road for us to leave the village by because the calèche didn't seem to have any brakes.

As we harnessed the horses in the morning, threading heads through collars and untangling bridles, I asked Edouard about brakes, which I hadn't yet discovered, and he agreed we had none. My mind boggled. We don't need brakes in Tana, Edouard explained logically. We can simply avoid the hills. No calèche had ever before been beyond its environs. If we had to go down the big hill he suggested lashing the spare wheel flat to the ground under a back wheel, but the strain could break the calèche. Normally you slow by making the horses lean back in their harness, but I doubted their hindquarters could cope with the gradient.

The villagers were mesmerised by the calèche and even more entranced by the horses. The lads rather liked the attention and didn't mind when they were elected as human brakes, using ropes tied to each back corner. Fortunately, there was a less steep road we could follow for our departure, and at the bottom of the hill the lads jumped aboard with another man to whom we gave a lift for several kilometres. He was bragging away about something and behind his back one lad called him 'a big goose which lays small eggs'.

Back on the level, I had another driving lesson. Edouard warned me to take the corners wide not tight or we would overturn. 'And don't try to make the horses trot until the calèche is rolling faster. Wait until a small slope in the road makes the carriage pick up speed, and then push into a trot.' So I practised letting the stagecoach help the horses along.

Horses have always been my favourite method of transport. Normally, I buy one in a market and travel with it, but I had long wanted to learn to drive a pair.

From the open hills of the high plateau we moved into a forest area along the edge of the escarpment where the backbone of Madagascar drops steeply towards the east coast, cantering gaily along a flat red track, slightly damp from dew and overhung with feathery mimosa trees and yellow and mauve flowering bushes that smelled pungent when the calèche brushed against them.

'You can tell the male trees from the female,' said Roland. 'The female leaves are thinner and longer and the bark is white, whereas the males have russet bark. The males grow faster and bigger.' He was proving to be a worthy guide, showing interest in all things. A big butterfly with black and yellow markings flew over my shoulder into the stagecoach and sat on the saucepans until a heavy jolt sent it fluttering out the window. The horses refused to cross a small stream but Edouard coaxed them calmly forward, then we followed the bank of a big river laden with red silt from the eroded hillsides. We crossed that river on a long open bridge without even a handrail, just the bare road and a swirling torrent below, but the horses took it in their stride.

At clearings in the forest people were making charcoal ovens. I could hear wood being chopped and see the smoke of fires above the trees. Horse 2 cast a shoe and we stopped at the next oven clearing. Charcoal-burners chop the coppiced branches into two-metre lengths and pile them into stacks with the thickest wood at the base, which are then left to smoulder under a cover of turf sods for a week. They calculated that a stack two metres wide and three metres long by one and a half metres high would produce twenty-two sacks of charcoal, selling at 2,250 fmg (Malagasy francs) per bag. What price a forest, I wondered, though it was less shocking to see charcoal-burners here because the real forest had already gone and they were only using eucalyptus which was planted for the purpose and regrows quickly.

Edouard made a deft job of reshoeing but admitted the metal was so weak shoes did not last long. I noticed the shoe turns up at the front to protect the toe. Back on the road, I took the reins for a spell and mulled over the pleasures of not having a motor, not only because of the fuel crisis but for the silence, broken only by clopping and creaking.

A chill wind blew up with dark clouds, and the men started making gloomy forecasts about the weather. At roadside houses, dogs rushed up barking which the horses ignored since they were used to it. But the moment the dogs realised they didn't recognise these particular animals they turned and backed off hastily. Rain swept across, as threatened, and I flicked the horses into a faster trot. We crossed a provincial boundary. Our route for the next few days would continue south. There were fountains of bamboo, hibiscus bushes in red flower, and five sets of cascades where our road met another tributary. The driving posed no particular problems and there was room to get past the frequent landslides.

By noon that day we were in a broad valley which produced good clay for bricks, said Roland, so people here built bigger houses. The village of Sabotsymanjakavahoaka lay some distance ahead but along the valley people lived in family smallholdings. At one house a man was wedging sandbags on a loose piece of roofing. Roland said it was futile. The wind speed in Cyclone Geralda had reached 250–350 k.p.h. It broke decades of world records. That was last month, February. In January there had been Cyclone Daisy which caused its share of devastation; so far this season thirteen cyclones had hit Madagascar, with lesser or greater damage.

We were still in the aftermath of Geralda, which left an estimated 500,000 people without homes, destroyed crops and hit the island's only oil refinery and put it out of action, and wrecked the country's major railway, linking the capital to the main port at Tamatave. Panic-buying had emptied the shops of foodstuffs with little prospect of resupply for some time, and queues of cars at petrol stations were two days long. Water supplies were cut off, all major roads were blocked by landslides and fallen bridges, and communication between the capital and provinces which was difficult at the best of times, was nil.

Cyclones are particularly bad news for a country as poor as Madagascar. The international community had responded quickly and generously to Geralda but the country was still in crisis and people seemed resigned to it.

The wind gusted and a rain storm broke overhead as we reached Sabotsy village, so we took shelter. Also taking shelter was a schoolteacher and his pupils, some of whom had five kilometres to walk home. The teacher introduced his two best students, aged eleven and fourteen, and said they excelled in literature and natural science. In fact Malagasy are often gifted in the arts. When I asked to hear the best singer, a girl was pushed forward and before she had time to be timid she sang her favourite song to us in a sweet tone.

I had lunch at the President of the Fokontany's house. He and his wife were elderly and he had only three teeth left, but his importance showed in his good manners and dignity. I put out my hand to shake hands and he took it between both his in a traditional Malagasy greeting.

The walls of the main room had a picture of President Zafy, a photo of their son's wedding, and a calendar of a girl on a beach with her bikini transformed by biro into a respectable dress. There were some hooks for spare clothes, a couple of wooden chests with padlocks, a table, chair and bed. The position each object occupies in a house or hut is generally dictated by tradition. The husband's bed usually goes along the east wall and the place for guests to sit is in the north or north-west. The hearth, water-pot and rice mortar have set places to the south and west, and objects of ceremonial use or family souvenirs go in the sacred north-east corner.

In Malagasy culture, astrological time and place come together in the home. By counting the twelve lunar months round the house's four walls and corners, starting with Alahamady in the north-east and going clockwise one can see the circulation of *vintana* in the various dimensions of time. This is why there are no round huts in Madagascar. The different months tell people what conduct and behaviour to adopt, in a way that is more complex than living with a Filofax.

For lunch we ate sugared manioc, then rice and a delicacy of zebu hump which was fatty but tasty. I was amazed at the amount of rice I was eating these days. The lads ate even more. It's said that Malagasy eat more rice per head per day than even the Chinese.

The schoolteacher, Naivo, turned out to be the son of the village President, and, because we had arrived at the end of term, he was delegated to help me get to know the area. The local economy is based on wood for house doors, shutters, floors, roof supports and balconies. I particularly liked the way many balconies throughout the region had carved ornamental balustrades. They were not wood-turners but the boards which formed the balusters were intricately dagged to make curved or zigzag diamond patterns which gave a delicate lace-doily effect. In general, one end of the balcony is used for washing purposes, letting the water drop away through gaps in the planking.

Naivo took me to see wood-cutters at work. We threaded single file across a kilometre of paddy dykes, mazelike with upright marker sticks denoting blocked or damaged paths, then up into once forested hills. Very little good timber remains, the stumps were only the regularly coppiced eucalyptus, and men would have to walk a long way to cut down a decent sized tree. After crossing some empty clearings, the sound of rhythmic sawing reached us and we arrived to find a two-man saw in use cutting a tree trunk into planks. One saw-man stands on the high platform which holds the log and the other stands below pulling and guiding the saw and getting showered in sawdust for his pains. The upper man slipped a wedge into place after every half-metre to hold the plank steady. Then their lean muscled bodies resumed the rhythm of the saw strokes. It was a tough way to earn a living.

Sadly, four-fifths of Madagascar's original forest has gone and the rest is fast being felled for firewood or building poles, or to clear ground for grazing and agriculture, felled by an exploding population struggling to subsist. But despite the appalling de-forestation Madagascar is a big island, fourth largest in the world, and its remaining forests still contain 10,000 named and countless unrecorded species of plants. Naturalists have only just realised they have hardly begun to document the forest's bio-diversity.

As for wildlife, the country is still called a living museum of natural history, an evolutionary laboratory. Part of the lost-world feeling comes because the island split off from East Africa's tectonic plate at the end of dinosaurs and the beginning of mammals. The flora and fauna evolved in isolation, and natural selection made different choices – as with the chameleons I'd seen, Madagascar contains more species than the rest of the world put together.

Ninety per cent of the island's plants and animals are found nowhere else in the world. Unknown life still waits to be discov-ered, one hopes before it becomes extinct or is destroyed by the inexorable march of deforestation.

With modern history's heavy human impact much of the giant wildlife has gone. A chicken was scratching for grubs at the side of the track, the same size as the smallest of the elephant birds which may still exist in Madagascar's unexplored recesses. The giant elephant bird roamed in dry savannah because it couldn't fly, and it shared its habitat with humans until hunted to extinction a few hundred years ago. It was easy prey, standing three metres tall on its elephantine legs, the largest bird that ever lived on earth.

One of its eggs could contain as much as 200 hen eggs. I looked at the chicken and tried to imagine an egg big enough to make seventy omelettes. Pieces of the shell, and sometimes whole eggs turn up occasionally in the south. When Marco Polo reported an island where a giant bird was able to pick up and carry the heaviest of beasts, he was probably referring to the elephant bird of Madagascar. In fact the name Madagascar may have come from Marco Polo confusing the island with Mogadishu, on the East African coast. Other theories about the name are that it means Island of Ghosts, or Island of Ancestors.

Keen to maintain his reputation as a source of local information in the face of a ghost-like rival, Roland told me about a ghostly bird living in caves to the south. A friend of his father was among those who had often seen it. They said it flew at night and there was light glowing out from under its wings, just a warm glow you could see with each beat of its wings, and it was brighter when it flapped hard. Of course it sounded absurd, except when you realised the caves where it lived were part of a uranium mine.

Our tour of inspection ended at a sacred stone, a small claw shape protruding only half a metre from the earth which had been swept back tidily in a square plot around it. The stone had given its name to the region, Naivo said, 'It is called Ambatodsdiaratsy which means the Stone-who-doesn't-like-Wrong-doers. In the past we used to leave a sweet or some other small gift on it and make a wish, but now,' he shook his head sorrowfully, 'some people do not respect the stone and have used it to sharpen their knives.' He showed me the marks in its claw-like curve.

When Roland asked in the village for information about the route ahead we were told it was fraught with obstacles and at least two bridges had been washed away. Cyclone warnings were going out on the radio. It could rain for days. It was already raining anyway, but not hard, so I suggested we travelled on that afternoon to Alarobia village to see if we couldn't get through. We were all prepared to press on and, at worst, we could change our route after the next night stop. If we had not worked out already that we had taken on a rather more serious bit of travel than any of us had expected, we knew it now. One should never assume.

3

We could do with extra muscle if the stagecoach got stuck and since Naivo knew the local conditions, I hired his services for two days. As we jolted along in the rain he explained to me some of the *fady* (taboos) of his people. 'You'll find that our traditions are taken seriously,' he said. Indeed I had already noticed that within only 100 kilometres of Tana, the capital, I seemed to have stepped back 100 years into the past.

No pork can be taken into certain villages, nor can people who have recently eaten pork be allowed into them. The most holy day of the week is Thursday; people are prohibited from working in the fields on Thursdays, though permitted to do so on Sundays, a case of the old traditional religion winning out over the imported Christianity.

This being rice harvest time, various extra *fady* were in operation for such an important crop. The harvest would be spoiled if people transported stones or building materials. I thought this might be because they should not waste their energy on such tasks just before a busy harvest time; but Naivo explained it was *fady* because the noise and shouting disturbs the rice itself. And bad weather will destroy your crop if you go gathering marsh grass for matting or thatching; to ensure the best harvest you should keep your house in order, sweep the floors, and abstain from eating certain vegetables.

Even the calèche lads, Tana town boys the pair of them, scrutinised the paddies, frowning with disapproval when they saw poorly developed rice. The correct timing of flooding and drainage is vital to a good crop. They quoted the proverbs, 'Good soil is wasted on a rice-field with too much water', and 'For every rice seed you plant you will harvest a hundred'. In addition, rice represents the toil of the ancestors so, as such, is holy. The toil of the present is the continuation of the past.

Continuity plays an important cultural role in Madagascar, a belief that the past and future are inextricably entwined together to form the present moment.

With an appalling lurch the stagecoach fell sideways in a hole and one wheel came high off the ground. We all instinctively threw our weight to the high side and the carriage dropped back into place.

They all said gosh it's getting dangerous, so I responded nonsense it's all quite normal. In truth, the muddy patches were dire, but when the lads faltered at such places, I said it was nothing compared to the mud in Africa. Perhaps we should pray, someone suggested.

As we lurched and slithered along Naivo bravely carried on talking about what people did instead of working on Thursdays. 'That's when people meet at the sacred place to celebrate the ancestors. They play the accordion and they dance. I don't myself, of course, because I am a teacher and a Christian, but there aren't many proper Christians in this region. A fair number observe both religions with the idea that two is twice as strong as one, or if one Almighty power is too busy to hear you, the other may listen. The state of the world today, anything is worth trying,' he concluded apologetically, going on to explain how the Christian God was equated with Andriamanitra 'the Fragrant Lord' and Andriananahary 'the Creator'. Sermons in church, no matter how long, fitted in with the native tradition of oratory, and the ancestors were like angels, as messengers between humans and God.

In this area in particular, the Christian church seemed never to have been welcomed, and many villagers contested its right to install itself. We passed near the grave of an English missionary family. Richard Champ had tried to evangelise the area early in this century and had been murdered, his wife and child along with him, and buried in the same grave.

King Radama 1 had initially encouraged Christian missionaries from the interdenominational London Missionary Society, the first being two young Welshmen, Bevan and Jones, and their families in 1818, though within a few months all but Jones had died of fever. Jones returned in 1820, followed by a handful of other missionaries, Welsh, Scottish and English. Over the next fifteen years they opened many schools and chapels, made many Christian converts, produced the first dictionary of the Malagasy language and translated the Bible into Malagasy. Some of the missionaries were craftsmen who taught Malagasy apprentices their skills as blacksmiths, carpenters, printers and weavers.

King Radama died quite young and was succeeded by his widow Queen Ranavalona I who was known as the Murderous One. We know a lot about what happened at her court because her private secretary had been one of several boys sent to England by Radama to be educated. He wrote several major historical manuscripts and kept a journal, mostly disapproving of the Queen's actions, writing in English so that nobody could read it. Ranavalona felt that Malagasy traditional culture was being threatened by Christian evangelism and within a few years she prohibited Christian practices and compelled the missionaries to leave. Christians who refused to recant were persecuted and many were slaughtered in various ways – speared or stoned to death, burned alive or thrown off the cliff outside the Queen's palace. But it was not only the Christians who were on the receiving end of her short sharp shock treatment. In a wave of terror in the 1850s, witches were denounced and thrown into boiling water, people who confessed to stealing chickens were sold into slavery and those who stole cattle were fettered in irons for life, in chain gangs of maybe six slaves. They had to keep dragging their dead comrades' irons until the last one died. Because of this many people fled their homeland and went to live in the forests of the east or the semi-desert lands to the west.

When the Queen threatened to apply the fierce Malagasy laws to European traders, British and French warships bombarded the port of Tamatave. In retaliation the Queen banned foreign trade and expelled all foreigners except for her favourite (and possibly at one time her lover), a French architect Jean Laborde who had been shipwrecked on his way back from India. He was a remarkable jack-of-all-trades who set up foundries and factories producing just about everything from cannon and rifles to candles and sealing-wax. He also built the great wooden Queen's Palace which was later enclosed in stone by a Scottish missionary and still dominates the capital city.

The ban on foreigners was finally lifted in the 1850s after the traders of Mauritius paid a humiliating fine. One of the first foreigners to appear, travelling up from the coast through the mountains where we were trotting, was the intrepid woman explorer Ida Pfeiffer. She was an elderly Austrian *frau*, who had already made her way twice round the world, often on foot. She reached Tana in 1857 when the Queen's persecution had reached such bloody heights that her son Prince Rakoto was driven to scheme with Laborde to dethrone her. Ida Pfeiffer became unwittingly drawn into the plot as she was staying at Laborde's house, and when the conspiracy was exposed she, along with all other Europeans, was put under house arrest and threatened with the death penalty. Prince Rakoto, who was spared because of his mother's love for him, persuaded the Queen to let the Europeans go and so Ida, Laborde and the rest were expelled and sent under escort to the coast. The guards were instructed to go the longest way via the unhealthiest places, and indeed the eight-day journey took them over fifty days and involved appalling suffering. Frau Pfeiffer survived to write her book but her health never recovered and she died a year later.

We passed through a village with a church atop its hill. Every village has a church, Catholic or Protestant, sometimes both. Missionaries had been allowed in again after the Queen died in 1861. They included French Jesuits, Anglicans, Quakers and Lutherans, which must have confused the Malagasy, especially as they tended to intrigue against each other in a most unchristian way. But the London Missionary Society, benefiting from being first in the field, was the most successful and its brand of Christianity became the official religion when the Prime Minister and his second queen-wife, Ranavalona 11, became converts in 1869. This meant that they had to conform to the LMS's strict puritanical standards and the Prime Minister had to divorce his original wife (before he started marrying queens) who had borne him eleven sons and five daughters. Curiously, he had no children by any of the three queens he married.

I asked Naivo about his own view of village life and he said it has always been based on the solidarity of the community. 'If people hold together like stone there is cohesion, not as grains of sand blowing forever apart.' Old people used to speak in proverbs regularly, he added, and there are still orators (*kabary*) who do this at *hira-gasy* music parties, using innuendo and witty double meanings, 'But it is a tradition we don't have much time for now,' he concluded, regretfully contemplating the way that civilisation seems to disintegrate under the pressures of modern life.

By evening we had reached a particularly pretty region, almost like being in a watercolour painting with the fading light casting patterns over scalloped rice paddies. It was too cloudy for a sunset, there was just a strange glow in the pink and black sky.

And it was raining harder. I suggested we should stop and camp rather than get stuck in the darkness but there was no way the men would agree to camp out. They said they would keep going, even if we arrived after dark, not only because of the rain but they were adamant the area was stiff with bandits. I said look there's four of you adult men, that's surely equal to any army, but the lads weren't keen and we toiled on.

With all this rain the road was rather slippery; where the laterite was soft it sogged into a morass, and where it was hard and smooth it had a very greasy film of mud. The rain gulleys had washed diagonally across the road making deep and awkward ruts. Our progress was painfully slow. The valley broadened and its sides became terraced with maize, manioc and pineapples whose fruit grow on the end of a long stem, as if being offered up.

The worse the track became, the more optimistic I appeared, perhaps because the lads were looking so horrified. I told them they were getting a good training. They were too apprehensive to ask for what. Squashed on a ledge between a long cliff of rock and a vertical drop we had further trouble, there being an almost impassable stretch of deep mud and large boulders. The evening grew chilly and I rummaged in the back of the calèche for my sweater. Suddenly I went flying and my arms hit the roof as the calèche swung and sank sideways. Two wheels came clear of the ground and the other two sank deep in a hole.

We were well and truly bogged down. We leapt out and cleared a channel to drain away the wettest mud, and tried to jack up the calèche to bring the wheels back to the ground. Then we ordered the horses into motion with me in the driving seat and

Edouard at their heads, while Naivo and the lads threw their weight to level the carriage at the moment when the horses pulled.

And so we continued, me driving between the bad bits and passing the reins to Edouard for the nasty moments. When I asked how far it was to Alarobia he said you'll see it just round the next corner, and every time he pointed I saw a different distant village. Nothing improved; it was tough for the rest of the route.

Our arrival in Alarobia did not bring the normal boisterous welcome, in the rain and the dark we attracted no attention. We heard afterwards that people thought we were raffia traders, using horses because the fuel shortage had worsened in Tana or the road was impassable except to horses. The latter was probably true. Raffia traders are common here and the locally woven mats are sold throughout Madagascar, not only for use on floors, but embellished with Christian slogans or local proverbs they are often pinned on the wall beside the bed.

Thanks to Naivo having friends in the village we were loaned an empty house to lodge in. The manners and perhaps the curiosity of the house-owner Armand meant he and his family came to stay too. They turned into charming companions. Armand worked for the Ministry of Agriculture but by nature he was a poet.

For twenty years he had been writing poetry, though sometimes he had no paper to write on, and had thrown away most of his early work. But he still had one exercise book densely written, every page neatly filled. His subjects reflected his professional preoccupations. 'Presence of Spirits' was a politically oriented poem about how farming peasants do not understand they are not producing enough to live by; other poems warned against soil erosion and bad husbandry and lamented the forest birds and creatures that are gone for ever.

A growing awareness of this devastation over the past fifteen years had made his soul cry out, a cry for what has disappeared, and an anger for the deforestation and erosion. So he encased his feelings in poetry to animate those who would listen. Against peasant ignorance he wrote:

Bordering the road and in the fields,
in the hill and around the yard,
there are plants flowering marvellously;
you don't really understand or know them.

The farmer doesn't understand that plants have needs,
requirements, and they can have illnesses.
Plants need air, sun, water, warmth,
and the wind to carry their seeds away
but peasants don't understand that plants rely on such
    things.

He read several poems aloud by candlelight, scanning and rhyming in Malagasy in four-line verses. 'In the Night' was a poem with soft-sounding words but staccato t, d, k, interspersed with lots of long urring syllables. Roland translated in part, while the wind started to gust and to rattle the tin roof. This was backed by the noises of the storm and dogs snarling outside, children playing underfoot and the lads next door clanking the cooking pots.

Poems such as one in praise of wheat reflected his work for the Ministry of Agriculture, which had introduced wheat to the area in 1983 as a winter crop rotating with summer rice. He told me 'Words are like rice plants and must be carefully arranged.'

'When does your inspiration come along?' I asked. He seemed too busy for poetic meditation.

'Oh, doing the rounds, visiting the local villages, I may see something which strikes me. It could be during a discussion by the roadside or in the mountains, the idea for a poem just comes into my head and in the evening, when I have time, I write it down.'

'Does it worry you if you do not have any paper?'

'No, not at all.' He was disarmingly genuine. 'But if I have a scrap of paper I scribble words all over it like a *bouillon* (soup). The day I got the inspiration to write 'This Changing World' I was walking along the road in the midday sun, on a four-hour walk, and as I reached the crest of a hill I could see some mountains with rocky sides and a great waterfall, while the peasants were sleeping, and the scene filled my spirit with such emotion that I sat and wrote the poem.'

When I asked why he had thrown his poems away he said he saw no point in keeping them. We talked on while the dogs barked outside in the rainy windy night. His favourite proverb was: 'If you plant a tree you can sit in its shade when you grow old.'

During supper with Armand I learned that elders should always stop eating before the young, so as to leave enough for them, and when we were served a mug of water he said that because I was elder he must wait to drink from it after me. Also, as part of the rules of seniority, I noticed that when people went past an elder, myself included, they mimed the tracing of a passage and asked to pass. It sometimes looked like exaggerated deference but in fact springs only from normal politeness and the *fady* that demands the gestures and words take place.

Armand's wife aged thirty-four already had eight children; it is not that family planning is not available, it is that children come from God and must therefore be welcomed.

It was nearly eleven p.m., I asked if rats would be a problem in the night and his wife said there were no rats, nor mosquitoes but probably a few fleas. She was right and I was frequently woken by the bites and by the cyclone winds that gusted with increasing force until the walls seemed to billow in and out. The roof above me sprang leaks in three places, so I moved over in my sleeping bag to fit between two sets of drips. And the fleas moved with me.

4

Morning brought a lull and since it was the weekly market day the tracks were thronged with zebu-carts and people wearing straw hats and carrying brimming baskets. After breakfast of wet-rice and egg I joined the market crowd. Besides fruit and vegetable stalls and the raffia traders for whom we had been mistaken, there were rabbits, guinea pigs and chickens on sale; freshwater crabs from a lake tied together on strings to prevent them scuttling away; wooden water troughs for livestock, and small tables selling home-made rat and flea poisons.

A whole section of the market was taken up by spade-sellers whose traditional long bladed spades were each inscribed with the emblem of their maker. The blacksmith section lured me over because the bellows-boys were using bicycle wheels to drive the airflow into each forge, and I watched axes being ground that were already worn almost to the butt. I ended up in the cattle and pig market and while taking temporary shelter from a rainstorm I met a young woman who told me that pigs are *fady* to her family. She pointed out beyond the village and said she used to go to the sacred ancestor place seven kilometres away but was forbidden to go there any more because she had got a job raising pigs. She was also banned from going to see her family because of the aura of pig, though her parents did visit her where she now lived with Armand's family in Alarobia.

From a hilltop I looked at the road east. As I had realised the previous day, a decision had to be made. This was as far south as we would get. The next village east was a big one topped by a church with spire, but the road had too many people on it and led to a well-populated lakeshore; we would take the emptier westerly way, back through Naivo's village to meet the north–south highway in a couple of days.

Our new route was known to be appalling and, with the past

twenty-four hours of rain, it could be quite a test. I held a conference with the crew before we set out, to make sure they were still willing and didn't want to run away. We all knew the going would be difficult. While saying goodbye to Armand I heard on his radio that the tip of the cyclone was spinning in our direction and could reach the area that afternoon. No point in hanging around so, despite the still pelting rain and wind, we harnessed the horses.

At first we tried to keep clean but within half an hour were soaked and muddy, the horses were muddy to their flanks; torrential rain lashed down, the elements were at work. We made steady progress. No one shirked or hung back when there was pushing to be done; in fact there was a distinct camaraderie developing as each tried to anticipate the other's needs. The Merina people are not slackers, they are known for hard work, thrift, patience, and a sunny nature.

One horse tripped and fell in mud to his chest. The horses particularly feared going into deep mud because they knew it could be deeper than expected. I could sympathise. Worse than being soaked and muddy was just not knowing where to put your feet, let alone the horses and wheels. I learnt a new word in Malagasy – mandrevou, which means bottomless mud. I began to wonder at what angle the calèche would finally tip over. Some of our near-disasters were very hairy. As for the crew, I hoped they would tell me if they reached their limit.

We couldn't get past a truck that lay bogged down and skewed sideways, leaving only a small gap between it and a bank that dropped down steeply in bushes, and in trying to manoeuvre past it one of the horses lost his balance and panicked. He broke away from the shaft and began toppling over the edge, still harnessed to the stagecoach. Momentarily Edouard blenched, unable to move. We had been through so much he was almost drained of reaction. But then he swiftly leapt to undo its traces and the horse jumped clear. It ran free, but we had our hands too full to worry, fighting to stop the weight of the calèche pushing the second horse over the brink. In terror it began to rear and tangle in the loose harness. We managed to release him too and I pulled him by the forelock to safe ground. I didn't want to let go but he kept prancing around, I feared that if both horses were loose they would run away; keeping hold of one meant the other would not stray far, and indeed he came galloping back, then closed in for a kicking battle with the one I was holding.

Meanwhile the lads were succeeding in edging the calèche around the truck and Edouard and I quickly reharnessed the horses to help them.

We continued on through streams, culverts collapsing, horses falling to their knees and bellies, and Edouard about to jump off to save his life. Yet among all these dramas, I was continually struck by the good manners of those we greeted along the way, and the various gestures by which they showed respect for each other. At noon we were nowhere, in pouring rain and ravenously hungry. I suddenly remembered the cake a friend had given me and now was a good time to share it.

Thunderstorms can be intensified or defused according to how you behave, I learned as we sat in the rain, munching vanilla cake, I also discovered that, as with so many other compartments of Malagasy life, there is a set of rules to govern human behaviour in storms. No whistling; no carrying of copper or iron, it challenges the storm; do not run away, the fast movement attracts lightning to follow; don't eat certain wild vegetables nor cut the young shoots of bamboo whose smell attracts lightning. Most of this made logical sense to me, and it meant the young bamboos would be protected from cutting until they became fine long poles.

To make a fetish against rainy weather you collect twigs from the Arify bush whose name implies clear dry air, some Honora grass, which means 'to roll up' (in this context 'to roll up the clouds', as it has power over the sky), a type of mimosa which drips resin from its branches and shavings from the Vavantana tree whose name means 'the mouth of the chameleon'. This is an allusion to the way the chameleon's sticky-tipped tongue lets nothing escape. In the same way the tree will prevent the rain-clouds from releasing the rain. Add in wet sand and dry it in a pot until all moisture has evaporated.

Fetishes also need prayer and ritual to make them effective, and the anti-rain prayer went something like this: 'Hear us! Andriananahary who canst bind the rain clouds so the sky will not press down on to the land, and the horizon will not be narrow. Let the rain clouds disappear.'

During the time the sorcerer is making this fetish he may not drink water, taking it only in food, and he must avoid walking on wet ground or wading across streams or puddles. It's at this time of year you would use such a thing, for the sake of the rice harvest.

Naivo said there was an elder nearby who was believed able to control hail storms and prevent them damaging the crops. He was also the spiritual chief of an annual ceremony of sacrifice up on the summit of a hill we were passing. 'Usually they kill a zebu for the ancestors, they don't skin it but eat it with the skin on.'

The next hill demonstrated the variety of faiths existing side by side in Madagascar. Naivo pointed out the cross on its summit. It was a Calvary to which the Catholics processed solemnly each Good Friday.

The landscape was growing rockier, strewn with large granite boulders. The next four bridges were all right but the river flowed in rapids of red mud. The road was much the same as a stream, with torrents pouring down it.

Trotting into Sabotsy, we chased a flock of geese along the main street and turned in under the arched entrance to the deserted marketplace. This is where Naivo lived and he took us to his house. Before entering, I emptied the water from my shoes and wrung out my clothes. I felt I was among old friends again. His three tiny daughters sat in a line watching me, and I gave them the photos to play with. Such things should be used until they fall apart from a thousand grimy hands. We sat in the same room, the row of girls, me writing my diary, and Naivo marking exam papers. He had been trying to teach his students about electricity, but since none of them had ever had the chance to use it, it meant little.

I couldn't find the desire to put on my wet clothes and set off into the afternoon rain. We had been tested enough in the morning and were all tired, so I decided not to move on until the morrow. We would need to cover forty-five kilometres, setting a fairly fast pace. One of the lads came in to consult about route and plans, and I said we would make a six-thirty a.m. start.

Naivo's niece of fourteen came in and stared with goggling eyes at me for a full hour without blinking. At last I asked what was the matter and Naivo said that I was her first white person, because she had never left the region nor seen television. Yes, she had seen pictures in a magazine, she whispered when I questioned her gently, but never in real life.

Europeans are not actually called 'white' because the colour white has offensive connotations. Tactfully, we are simply called '*vazaha*', or foreigner. To 'white' someone in Malagsy means to slander them, to 'spit white' means to fail in an appeal (usually to borrow money), and an unreliable person speaks 'white words'. The colour which for us stands for innocence and purity, implies all that is ugly and of low quality.

What did his niece think of her first foreigner? I asked. 'Very nice' she said diplomatically and still her eyes never left my face.

I took the worst of my wet gear to dry in the kitchen, up a wood ladder into the roof. The cooking hearth was raised up to worktop height on a base of clay. When I asked where the toilet was Naivo said it was in the south-west. He didn't say 'outside the front door on the left'. Sensibly, it had soft pumpkin leafed vines growing outside for practical reasons.

Roland told me about a *hira gasy* group that was due to visit the village and he explained that it involved a mix of discourse, sometimes in proverbs, music and theatrical performance. The *hira gasy* I went to had two competing groups, trying to outshine each other and win the appreciation of the audience, which they hoped would lead to bookings to play at village celebrations in the year ahead. There are hundreds of such groups on the high plateau, and they travel extensively to fill their engagements.

I found space to sit under a makeshift tarpaulin shelter out of the rain. The discourse seemed to be giving advice on life. The men wore red jackets with blue lapels and straw boaters, and looked as if dressed in 1900s French army uniform for a Colonial lawn party. Much applause greeted the women as they came into the open stage area, twelve dancers in a wide circle, singing lengthy obituaries and fluttering their hands at the crowd with much wagging of index fingers, in what were songs to warn people to behave in life and so become good ancestors. Old men and women danced together in a graceful way, though the prime dancers were two small boys who bobbed around kicking and stamping and twirling their waist-sashes, dancing with hands and feet, clapping above and below their knees, then kneeling and swing-kicking to face the other way.

The rain was collecting in the collage of tarpaulins overhead and every now and then a strong gust of wind tipped a puddle on to some unsuspecting head. Trumpets, drums and violins joined in, impervious to the rain, the drummers beating the metal sides of their kettle-drums in soldier-style. A man with a watering can came through the crowd, selling tea which he poured into tin mugs threaded on to the can's spout.

Every few minutes the dance circle moved round, turning so that a different dancer faced each part of the crowd. One was an elderly angel-faced woman with hair scraped tightly back into a bun, high cheekbones and long slim neck. The women wore calf-length pastel lacy dresses with long lacy shawls, puff sleeves and short overskirts. A couple of them held umbrellas, but the rest were soaked by the rain and deserved every bit of applause.

The dance was followed by an orator telling stories from current life which frequently made the crowd burst out laughing and throw back remarks, creating more laughter. A man in the audience shouted his admiration for a girl dancer and she replied, 'If you follow me home my family will beat you.'

The orator pointed at me and made remarks about my age, which I decided to take as a compliment because Malagasy respect their elders, and this was followed by more laughter.

Violent weather continued all night with the tin roofs in the marketplace in front of the house flapping crazily. The news was that the cyclone had killed twelve people and destroyed eighty per cent of the small town of Voemar to the north. It was now passing fifty kilometres east of us, swerving with the escarpment ridge and heading south losing power.

After breakfast of rice with manioc purée we climbed aboard the calèche and set off at a brisk trot from the village to a five-way crossroads. Naivo was with us for half a day longer, guiding us west down grassy hills and over a series of causeways across rice paddies. He pointed out how the irrigation was intricately linked using bamboo pipes and half-hollowed tree-trunk conduits over lower channels, keeping a steady trickle in many directions.

On terraces near houses it was time for planting manioc; all you have to do is stick twigs in the ground and they grow. Beside certain houses were round fenced enclosures with a pit inside, which Naivo explained are to keep zebu for fattening for the next *famadihana*. A bullock could be kept in there for six months from November when the cut grass starts being full of goodness; the pit is dug so that the animal has more protection against the chill winds of winter on the plateau. *Famadihana* is an expensive business, since a zebu costs 100,000–300,000 fmg, but each family needs to hold its bone-turning ceremony every three to seven years, and more often if it feels dogged with ill-luck.

Back in the stagecoach my bum was getting sore. The road had improved but we still had to navigate across broken culverts and gulleys, and at one point the calèche slipped nastily backwards dragging both horses. Their hooves scrabbled to find a grip, they slid another metre, out of control, and Edouard fell sideways as the carriage jolted hard against rocks and began to topple over. Again we leapt to the high side to restore the balance. The worst bridge of the day was a double span that had lost its planks. We loosed the horses and sent them through the river, then found planks to rebuild the bridge as far as the first pillar.

It was a question of rolling the calèche along and picking up the planks from behind to put in front. Being unsecured, if you trod on their ends they tipped. Below us was a foaming torrent. One plank twisted under the calèche's weight and slewed sideways, leaving us poised over a gaping hole. The carriage was about to fall, but in milliseconds one of the lads had thrown some wood across the gap and saved the day.

There are five sacred houses in this region. I stopped in Mangabay to look at one of them, but it was empty and since the owner was away I did not go inside. It was distinguished from the other houses in the village by crossed gable decorations and was set apart behind a fortified ditch. The girl with the pig *fady* problem whom I had met in Alarobia said that they were places that grow in power through weekly meetings with music and dancing which invoke the presence of the ancestors.

When I asked about the local economy I learned the area produces silk and raises silk worms, though the ones in this village had died when their mulberry trees were attacked by insects. Silk cloth woven from local cocoons is made into *lambas* and used to rewrap the dead bodies at the bone-turning ceremony.

Naivo had to leave us here. I said goodbye, knowing I had made a friend, and enjoying his smile of delight at his wages. Our desperate journey together had been a bonding experience. We had all worked hard in different ways and I had grown to appreciate Naivo's clear honest eyes and his eagerness to communicate whatever he knew of interest along the muddy way. Before I left Mangabay the elders invited me back for their bone-turning celebrations in three months' time. So we would meet again.

We were now heading for Roland's sister's house near Ambatofotsy. Ambatofotsy is on the plateau's north–south road and railway and was where I would regretfully part company with the calèche. But that was still thirty kilometres away and I was able to put the parting out of my mind while I enjoyed the day.

Our lunch break was in a grassy spot at the base of a ravine. Edouard fetched a bucket of water and the horses were so thirsty they both jammed their noses in together. Various people came along and stopped to look and offer advice about the route ahead. A small child came past leading a zebu with two sheep at his heels and a piglet trotting along behind. I had been messing about trying to crack Edouard's whip, but it was just too short, probably it had broken at the crucial place after a lifetime of being cracked. So I asked the boy with the zebu to lend me his whip to try. It worked better and I produced some decent cracks out of it. Then suddenly, out of the inevitable audience, a man leaped into the road, whirling and jumping as he cracked his whip in every direction in a machinegun-fire performance. What a display! I was hugely impressed. Then all the zebu herders in different valleys began replying to it with double and triple whip-shots, the sounds from far away carried on the wind.

The afternoon gave us a top-of-the-world feeling. We had climbed back to a high part of the plateau, where it was sunny and breezy, among open grassy hills with occasional houses tucked into narrow red eroded valleys.

Edouard was feeling the effects of a hard week, so he often gave me the reins now and I was content. I always enjoy driving horses, but had to remember to concentrate. I was talking so much at one point, we nearly hit a bank, and when we met a Land-Rover it gave me such a surprise I swerved automatically to the UK side of the road.

Late that day we came to an area of fortified villages, their defensive walls now in disrepair. Some homesteads were in a ruined state too, but others were still inhabited or partially inhabited in a tangle of garden weeds and creepers run amok and flowering with luscious drooping clusters of orange bells. The walled enclosures were seldom built adjacent with shared walls. When they were in groups they usually had enough space for a zebu-cart to go along between two properties. One of the most striking walled plots had two tall thin house-towers seeming to form a gateway, with a big dark house in the western corner, and another separate walled area spreading down the hill. This defensive lifestyle dated back to the feuding sub-kingdoms and patchwork states of the eighteenth century, and reflected the insecurities of olden times.

Walled villages like these can be found all over the high plateau around Tana. The most important ones had gateways with great solid wheels of stone that were rolled open and closed by the efforts of up to forty men. One of the most magnificent is at Amboimanga, with a diameter of over four metres, while at Ansadinta village there are also secret passages, some reserved for royalty. Though the gates were no longer there, I had once met a royal descendent who still slept in the last queen's bed. She showed it to me, a monstrous cumbersome wooden thing with wings.

I asked if it was comfortable and she said no it was much too hard, ever since the original base had fallen apart and they had replaced it with planks. But she was intensely proud of the bed and of the old queen's combs which she also still used.

Defensive walls are no longer necessary but the people still fear interference from the outside world. When I asked if they wanted better roads they said they didn't because it would bring an invasion of people and give easy access to robbers. Besides, the zebu-carts would lose work. I wondered if this innate fear of invasion was a manifestation of an island mentality, as contrasted with that of continental populations accustomed to a continual current of human movement.

Our journey had accomplished a good mileage and we pushed on, girding up the tired horses. Finally from a high ridge we caught sight of the railway and the town of Ambatofotsy, and on the outskirts we arrived at the house of Roland's sister. The horses needed a rest, as did the men.

Roland's mother came out to meet us, and we all gabbled away as if I had known this charming family for ever. Roland's brother-in-law was the only one strangely silent, then he apologised and said how much he wished he could talk but he was ashamed he didn't know enough French. Most people I had met could speak no French whatsoever. I had started learning Malagasy, but it was only basic. One of the problems for a beginner is coping with prefixes that change a root word from a noun into a verb or an adjective. And place names are especially formidable because they are built up of a number of descriptive details strung together to make one word. You expect them all to end with the Malagasy equivalent of 'You can't miss it'!

Sitting relaxing at last in Roland's sister's house, we talked over our best and worst moments, Edouard said the worst was when he made up his mind to jump off the runaway calèche, and the best was the happy way we had got along together throughout the journey.

I was given a bed which consisted of a mattress on top of a sheet of corrugated iron on wooden slats. It was a bit short for me. My feet hung over the end and when I turned over the slats moved and the whole bed collapsed, so at midnight I pulled the mattress away and rebuilt the bed, using the bridge-building techniques I'd learnt on the way, and wondered if the old queen had to do the same.

Next morning I would take the train back to Tana. The calèche lads helped me down to the railway station and they all came to wave goodbye.

TWO

Alahamady

5

Normally I dislike cities, I get a feeling that their inhabitants all know each other and know their way around and I don't. So usually I pass through urban areas at speed to get out the other side, but none of this applied to Tana. I felt welcome and somehow at home, thanks to the friendship and hospitality of Pascal Rakotomavo and his family whose town house was centrally located with a garden overlooking Lake Anosy. The city is built on a group of hills, and the old Imerina houses have picturesque rickety wooden balconies covered in flowering creepers. Old stone stairways interlink the town and some houses have no access to roads except by paths.

I had innumerable errands to carry out, applying for permits for my various destinations, finding out information about them; checking the music and arts currently in town, exhibitions and festivals, and arranging to give a couple of lectures for English language students. And I still had to find myself a horse to ride in the races. I wanted to enter a race at the next Grand Prix Cup. The season would not start for a couple of months, and I thought I could probably train in between my travels. The search for a racehorse proved lengthy and more complicated than I expected, but new doors kept opening. One weekend I went to the Rakotomavo family farm twenty kilometres from the capital.

This was rural life but in a totally different style from my calèche trip. Discreet floor bells under dining tables called for service from the kitchen, and my bedroom had a fireplace and lace tops to the sheets. Having closed the curtains, no daylight woke me and I overslept until mid-morning.

In the yard I found cattle, chickens, pigs, and horses. Pascal's best racehorse had been a mare sadly gored to death on the horns of a zebu; he had another mare with a two-week old foal and there were three smaller horses for me to try. Pascal's daughter Freddie said her brother Gino would take me for a long ride later on. My husband had known the Rakotomavo family for twenty-five years and I had made friends with Freddie a few years ago during her studies in Paris and London. She now had a job in Tana in a finance house, and was almost as good with figures as her father, a former Minister of Finance – which has to be a particularly thankless task in a Third World country.

One of the pleasures that Pascal had from the farm was his collection of orchids. Madagascar has over a thousand species of orchid and many are epiphytes, growing on the trunk of trees without needing soil, but living in harmony, not as parasites, and collecting water as it runs down the trunk. Some orchids have only one insect type that can pollinate their deep cups; some flower in chains a metre long. Pascal showed me his star orchids, white spiders, and slipper orchids with red spots, and alongside them, among the lilies, was a gorgeous frilly flower with petals in all shades of purple and violet. None of these came from nurseries. He had collected most of the plants himself while on camping trips and long duck-shooting weekends, others were gifts from a wide diversity of friends. It was Pascal who had first told me about an amazing region I planned to visit called the *tsingy*. He knew his Madagascar better than most capital city-dwellers.

At the end of the garden, bordering rice paddies, a travellers' palm was sprouting bird of paradise-type flowers. If it grew taller than the house, a fellow guest told me, it would have to be cut down. Nothing to do with suburban notions of damaging the foundations. If it outgrew the house it could bring death to those living there. On a more practical level, the heart of the palm is used to cure anorexia. Eating it gives you a huge appetite. Farmers also use it for fattening cattle. I loved the way traditional lore and medicine intertwined all the time in Madagascar and I loved Pascal's garden with the fruit trees newly harvested of their guavas, apples, pears and grapefruit. The seemingly haphazard arrangement of his planting with flowering creepers and tree ferns growing in a naturally pleasing way warmed me to the Malagasy appreciation of nature.

The horses were saddled and ready. I took a small brown stallion which hadn't raced for several years, with Gino on an elderly grey, and we rode through the village and out into the hills. The horses were fresh and we cantered easily on the red earth tracks. A long level stretch gave an excellent gallop. I took second place, tucking myself into the racing seat and tried to remember the instructions – bum up, nose down, almost into the horse's mane, jab your toes down in the stirrups, get your weight forward; it was a balancing act, my weight held between my knees and hands on the withers where I'd jockey-looped the reins. I found I couldn't hold the position for long and my balance was a little precarious. But I was pleased enough for the time being. I wondered about asking Pascal to lend me the horse to put into race training, but the practice circuit was a dangerously gulley-laced track and I was frightened of Pascal's valuable animal coming to harm. The horse was also smaller than I wanted. To have a sporting chance in the Grand Prix I would need the biggest possible mount.

I am not a professional jockey. My last ten-yearly effort had been in Papua New Guinea in the 1980s, and before that I had raced once in Lagos. Under Jockey Club Rules I don't even qualify as an amateur. When I applied to the Jockey Club of Madagascar for permission to ride, they said show us your prizes. I didn't like to say I had never won any.

Horses are not indigenous to Madagascar. The first ones were imported in the seventeenth and eighteenth centuries from Europe but were only of limited interest to the Malagasy nobility. In 1817 an Englishman James Hastie brought three horses, one of which was destined to be a present for the king, but it drowned in a river on the way to Tana. So the first Malagasy horsemen were the king's two younger brothers. The horses were so greatly adored by their royal masters that they quickly fell ill with indigestion from overeating. Hastie wrote that when he visited the invalids he found sacks of rice open before them and mangers full.

The king began riding lessons himself, holding in his mouth an amulet to protect him against harm. Afterwards he laughed, cried and danced with pleasure at the experience, and ordered his military staff to learn to ride also. More horses were requested from Britain. The next king Radama II was an intrepid cavalier and during his reign the breeding and training of horses grew in importance. The use of a lunge rein was called 'making the horse go around the moon'.

The mountain beyond where Gino and I were riding was the place where some of those first horses in Madagascar were stabled. King Radama's son and his Sakalava bride used to ride out here together. His tomb is on a nearby mountain and even now there are local people who claim his ghost can still be seen there on horseback. Pascal told me that once when he was riding near the tomb the late afternoon sun threw the long shadow of his horse on to the hillside and the people were very afraid.

After our ride the horses were washed down with cold water from the well. There is no running water supply in the village now, although there used to be when Pascal was a child. He said they found traces of a water course with a natural gradient down the hill connecting five villages. They put it back in running order, but within six months it fell into disrepair through lack of maintenance. Again it was repaired, and again damaged, it had not now worked for many years. There are people who earn a living by carrying water for households, and when running water comes to a village, they are out of a job.

A barbecue lunch party had been arranged for family and friends – home-made pâté de foie gras, a suckling pig basted with honey, and rice with a sauce of meat steamed with crabs from the paddies. The crabs give the meat a unique flavour; several Malagasy specialities combine fish and meat in this way. When Gino married a year ago, 300 guests had been invited. Gino said he would never have considered marriage outside his Hova clan. Among rural Malagasy the choice of marriage partners is further complicated by *vintana* – water, fire, wind, and hill – a bit like the medieval elements. Which element predominates depends on your *fady*; wind cannot marry hill because of conflict; fire can marry wind, they go well; but if fire marries water, the fire will be put out.

In pursuit of a bigger racehorse I went one morning to visit Gerard Ramanantsoa a professor of economics at the university who owned a lot of horses. His house was one I noticed when first I arrived in Tana this year because I had stayed a few days in a hotel opposite its forbidding garden wall. In the bustling street you only see the high wall but from my window I glimpsed a beautiful old house set among trees and flowers, an enclave of peace and birdsong amid the traffic and exhaust fumes.

The sophistication of so many Malagasy city folk makes Madagascar less like her African neighbours, perhaps because its history has always contained a structured hierarchy. Gerard was playing the piano when I arrived and when he offered me refreshment he said, 'I'm sorry I've only got alcohol.'

At ten-thirty a.m. it was a bit too early for me, and I busily revised my preconceptions about economics professors. Pieces of saddlery were hooked over sculptures and paintings, which were in turn mixed in with natural treasures collected over the years like polished ammonite and quartz crystals. Unfortunately, he had no racehorses, as he specialised in the jumping scene. There would be other leads. But time was passing and if I didn't find a horse to put in training soon, I might as well forget about racing.

Another delightful discovery was that a Malagasy friend Elie Rajaonarison, whom I had met in England two years before, was now Secretary-General at the Ministry of Culture. When he stayed at my farm he had helped me paint a huge scene of sky and clouds on a bedroom ceiling, teaching me how to put movement into the skyscape in a way few other people could have done and I now very much enjoy living with that painting. I had known Elie was also a poet, but he used to say every Malagasy has a deep sense of poetry, and everyone in Madagascar is a natural poet. In this he was undervaluing himself. Many people do not have the time to open their eyes and to feel sunlight passing on an earthen wall. But it was something Elie could capture and help them to pause and appreciate. 'Poetry keeps me feeling alive,' he said. 'When I was abroad the moonlight was never the same as here, and the sunsets made me sad because they were not the sunsets of Madagascar. Such simple things are easily set in verse.'

I spent a morning at Tsimbazaza botanical park and zoo where the chief of flora Sylvain Razafimandimbison walked me round talking about the uniqueness of the plants. Tsimbazaza is one of the more active and energetic of such institutions, frequently collaborating with Kew Gardens. Dr John Dransfield of Kew had recently identified a new species of palm tree and planted a seedling of it here at the park, adding to the genetic bank. The fruit has not yet been seen by botanists, though the villagers say it is small but edible.

My favourite plants for curiosity are the insect-eaters and Sylvain showed me some that eat insects, butterflies and even small birds. The leaves end in cup shapes as deep as nine inches, complete with lid which closes when a victim goes inside. In the rainy season the cups always have a bit of water in them and the insects that fall in quickly decompose, allowing the plant to absorb their nutrients. Another carnivorous type has rounded spiny leaves and, when a butterfly lands, the leaf quickly closes and impales its prey, like a supercharged sundew.

Back at Freddie's house her brother Gino was playing a heavy sonata on the piano, meaning he was waiting for Freddie and his wife Vivienne to be ready to go shopping. The couple had the nesting urge and needed to buy curtains, I hoped to buy a yellow shirt, and Freddie wanted to see an exhibition of locally produced materials from silks and cottons to jute sacking. So we all went off together.

Along the way we saw the other side of Tana life. As in any capital city, there is a jungle life of professional beggars and streetkids. Madagascar has spiralled down from the tenth to the fourth poorest country in the world. So for those unfortunates there are no jobs, no money for schooling, often not even a record of their birth. About two thousand people stay alive by picking through rubbish; those in the streets get first pickings and those at the municipal dump have to compete with scavenging pigs and dogs.

Over a thousand of these garbage pickers live beside the dump, and they have made tunnels deep into it looking for ten- or twenty-year-old garbage when people still threw away broken plates and worn out shoes. The night shift of pickers burn car tyres for light, producing lung-damaging smoke. Madagascar needs all the help it can get.

I gave something to an old man who had come out to beg in his Sunday best grey suit near the *zoma*. Tana's Friday *zoma* is reputed to be the world's second largest open-air market. (None of the guidebooks that make this curious point tells you which is the largest.) It sets up under a sea of tall umbrellas and sells most of life's necessities from vanilla and spice to single shoes and bent second-hand nails. In the handicrafts section there were leather and crocodile-skin bags and belts, decorative straw baskets piled in tall stacks, artefacts and jewellery made from cowhorn and tortoiseshell, semi-precious stone solitaire sets, made for the town and tourist markets, and all of good quality craftsmanship. There were musical instruments, too, like the *valiha*, which is a piece of hollowed bamboo with strings stretched lengthways down its outside to produce rippling chords. Among a collection of hand-made wooden models I swooped on two model calèches, almost identical to Edouard's, with a driver in charge of the reins, their insides full of country folk going to market and their roofs laden with baskets full of carved pineapples and squawking geese.

These were still the most reliable form of transport running. For about a week the whole city was on foot when the price of petrol went into crisis – not because of Geralda, but because the country's economy was in dire straits. The World Bank and IMF came for talks that forced Madagascar to float its currency, cutting its value in half before I left. This immediately raised the cost of fuel, and no one could afford it. Tana's whole taxi force went on strike. When petrol queues were seventy-two hours long, a good friend of mine put her car in the line nearest her company's office and worked from it with errand boys bringing her paperwork and phone messages. This was dearest Norososa Ranivamboahangy who was assigned to help sort out all my problems and office needs. She was a treasure in so many ways, though I sometimes felt guilty at adding to her in-car paperwork.

The Malagasy are known for having patience, as I saw in the massively orderly bus queues – very unFrench. In their last major revolution in 1992 they forced their President's resignation by non-violent demonstration. The whole country had gone on strike for nearly a year, economically crippling for a poor country. But being a bloodless revolution, there was little foreign news coverage at the time.

My feet often took me past the flower market on the way to appointments, just to enjoy the perfume, especially the frangipani, and the sparkling freshness of the roses and gladioli. There was

seldom an empty moment in my day. The friendship I was given
was not necessarily for my own sake. It showed people's affection
built up over twenty years for my husband. I enjoyed having
the chance to get to know those who before had only been
acquaintances.

Apart from meeting wonderful old Malagasy families in aca-
demic and business sectors, I also enjoyed going to diplomatic
dinners and other events including the Queen's Birthday celebration, a highpoint in British Embassy life in such faraway
places. There was a brass band and a lawn party of amazing
elegance and medals of honour and speeches by the British
Ambassador Peter Smith, who clearly cares deeply for Madagascar
and works tirelessly for the benefit of Anglo-Malagasy affairs,
and by my friend Herizo Razafimahaleo, the dynamic leader
of a political party called the Non-Political Party. He was
the current Minister of Tourism and Industry, and had just
come up with the slogan – 'Madagascar, the world's best kept
secret'.

Madagascar might be a forgotten part of the world, but I
noticed the number of international aid agencies in action there
had increased in both conservation and humanitarian fields, with
an impressive start made by FAO's David Fletcher who flew in
the face of convention using ingeniously successful methods to
organise emergency aid to the drought-ridden south. It is not
easy to turn imaginative ideas into reality.

In pursuit of my racehorse I continued to encounter technical
problems because of my lack of jockey credentials. Grand Prix
jockeys were professional and my only hope seemed to be a
race open to 'Gentlemen Cavaliers and Amazons'. It was such
a delightful title and I hoped I qualified in the second category.
I went to meet an elderly gentleman cavalier who agreed I could
compete as an Amazon. The only trouble, as he delicately pointed
out, might be assembling a field to race against. He and his aged
peers were now *hors de combat* and none of the young seemed
interested. He obviously adored his horses which were almost as
old as he was. During the last cyclone when the floodwaters had
lapped his front door, he had brought them into his house and
installed them in the living-room.

My newest contact was a young woman called Ange whose
father had been involved in racing and kept several racehorses on
which Ange had learned to ride. Her love of horses came because
when she was a child her mother banished her to spend the night in
the stables when she was naughty. She didn't want to race herself,
however.

'Too fast, too dangerous,' she said. I asked if jockeys used dirty
tricks and she said of course, it was normal everywhere, wasn't
it?

'They could give a horse some aspirin which makes it sweat,
or give it cold water before it runs. Watch out at the start that
someone doesn't try to injure your horse, and in the race they'll
bump into you, of course. It's normal. You have to get a good
start. If you are behind, another jockey may stick his whip up
your horse's nostrils when you try to come alongside. Oh, and
watch out for fallers, they're always a hazard.'

Ange could hardly be called encouraging, but my mind was
still set on my competing. So my training continued out at the
farm with Gino and we had some fabulous gallops in the dusty
hills. It was true that I never won any of them, until one day
on Pascal's old grey mare. It was my turn to call 'Go' and I
delayed the start. Instead of beginning at the foot of a rutted
hill, I nursed the mare up it and, when the horses' noses were
level at the top, I yelled 'Go!'.

The mare's hind legs cannoned out and we launched into
a flat-out gallop. I took the lead at a slight left bend. Gino
challenged but the mare extended her stride and, though twice
more he tried to overtake, she simply ran even faster. It was
like flying. The track ended in a T-junction where you have to
swing sharp left, which is as good a way of stopping as any. At
last I had won a race of sorts.

The racing calendar finally announced that the season would
start two months late this year. It gave me some welcome lee-
way. Time for more travelling.

6

I headed south by train to the end of the line, passing the mountains where I'd travelled by calèche and the railway station where we'd said goodbye. Where I was going next there were no roads for my trusty calèche, not even cart tracks, only steep footpaths. The end of the line was the old French colonial town of Antsirabe where I planned to stay the night before heading on down to the Zafimaniry wood-carving region for a four-day walk.

Emerging from the handsome 1930s railway terminus I strolled along a broad boulevard past the hot water spa whose healing properties had first put the town on the map. Various missionaries and monasteries had settled here, the climate being cool and the soil rich and fertile. I went to the Catholic convent to meet a young English doctor and his nurse wife, Oliver and Camilla Backhouse, who I had first met in London when they were planning to put a year of their lives into medical work in Madagascar. I admired their resolve. They certainly needed it. Oliver, an eye specialist, had succeeded in finding work in Antsirabe's Lutheran hospital. The surgery to remove cataracts is cheap, quick, and produces rewarding results. Most of his blind patients had not been able to see their families for years and when their sight was restored he said they didn't cry with joy, they laughed. To be able to watch people walk away, their sight restored, marvelling to see the world around them, makes one envy Oliver his ability to bring such happiness.

He had been doing up to fifty operations a month, in rural dispensary rooms where, before each operation, they began by swatting the flies. The couple showed me round the small neat hospital. This time of year was especially troublesome for eyes, since the dust from threshing rice exacerbates the corneal ulcers that, if untreated, can lead to blindness.

Many children suffer from xerophthalmia, a blindness due to Vitamin A deficiency. The area easily grows carrots, mangoes, papaya and tomatoes but they are not eaten by the local people, just sold as a cash crop. Malagasy will eat rice or cassava three times a day. One woman the Backhouses went to see had nine children, four of whom were blind with xerophthalmia – and her income came from growing carrots which she sold to buy rice, or fed to fatten the pigs. Another woman brought in three of her children with gonococcal eye infections, which they treated and, because it is infectious and recatchable, they gave her some medicine for the other children at home. Soon she was back, having sold the medicine to buy rice. Oliver and Camilla were not optimistic about the co-ordination of health education programmes in a country suffering such rock-bottom poverty. Injections are not the easy answer when needles are so blunt they bend against the skin, and arms already have abscesses from dirty needles. Ollie and Camilla were starting a system whereby before leaving the island western travellers to Madagascar could donate any unfinished medicines they would not need back home to Mad Optique in central Tana, for distribution to those in need. Of course the medicinal properties of Madagascar's huge range of curative plants are in international demand. The most sensational of these has been the rosy periwinkle, used to cure childhood leukaemia. It is now saving the lives of four out of five patients it is used on. When one considers the millions of dollars being made by Western drug companies processing this herb, it seems grossly unfair that no royalty or patent fee is payable to the island which is the only original source of supply.

Ollie and Camilla arranged for me to stay the night at the convent where they were lodging. To summon one of the sisters they use a bell system whereby each sister has a number. No. 4 was four clangs on the old brass bell, and No. 14 was one then a pause, then four. I was soon installed in a room labelled Joan of Arc.

The couple had just been joined by another British doctor Peter Jay, whose irrepressible humour even survived the local flea infestation. I shared their farewell dinner at the convent, as they were all going to work at a leper colony for the next two months. It was also somebody's birthday, so we had a cake with a candle on it. Next morning we drove south together in their ancient Land-Rover to the town of Ambositra, and stayed at a hotel where at the end of the evening, instead of closing up, the staff started laying out their bed mats on the floor of the bar while we sat talking and drinking the local wine. We watched the girls brushing their hair, curling it in squiggles, instead of rollers, and wrapping themselves in a head-cloth before settling down for the night on the bar floor rather than face a long dark walk home.

It was difficult to find transport on to Amtoetra on the border of the Zafimaniry wood-carving region. The village was so remote that nothing went there except on the weekly market day. Eventually, despite the fuel crisis which still meant petrol rationing and queues, I hired Rakoto and his ancient jalopy. He needed the money to support his seven children, aged five to eighteen. His wife had died soon after the seventh was born. As we left we saw three of his children dressed for Sunday church and stopped to give them a coin each for the collection.

The road to Amtoetra was not bad but slow and flooded. The car, being twenty years old, regularly threatened its last gasp, particularly as we wound up into the mountains. Beyond Amtoetra there were no roads. My walk would go scrambling around on the outer face of the escarpment above the eastern coastal plain; as the crow flies, perhaps only 100 kilometres from the ocean.

In Amtoetra I bargained over food supplies and rates for a guide and porter, intending to walk for four days. I was not so fortunate this time as I had been with Edouard and his team. The first sign of trouble from my guide and porter was a stream of complaints that they were hungry. It was only ten a.m., but they said they hadn't had any breakfast. I gave them some bread, said we would picnic at noon, and pressed on.

In crossing on to the exposed windward elevation the weather changed; low clouds coming up from the coast gathered over us and began drizzling, and the narrow path became alternately a stream and a waterfall. My shoes squelched along, but warmly enough, it was a sweaty day, over open moorland uplands, deforested by slash and burn agriculture, and in the breeze I could hear the music of a zebu herder playing Pan's pipes. Up and down hills we trailed, balancing over deep streams spanned by slender rolling logs, and took our midday halt on a big bald granite outcrop beside Mount Afaliarivo, the highest summit in the region which loomed, steep-sided and craggy, before vanishing in the clouds blowing up from below.

On the outcrop were some crosses and standing stones. The latter are fairly common throughout Madagascar, but I could get no proper information about these ones because Silberb and Co, the guide and porter, did not know enough words to explain in French, nor did they have any interest in the meaning or history of such objects. Silberb thought the cross with aloes growing round its base might be in remembrance of a wood-carver extraordinaire who had lived in the village where we were aiming to spend our first night. We pressed on.

The path was not a route for the faint-hearted or those with vertigo, and I was quite glad of the low cloud blotting out the drop which was sometimes sheer on both sides. Out of the mist loomed sprays of giant bamboo, their base thick with new growth of metre-long tightly furled bamboo spikes. Waterfalls on both sides meant my ears were hearing different rhythms, coming and fading individually with each valley but in stereo. The rock foot-holds were covered in algae and slippery from the continual rain. I fell once, stopping a few inches from the edge, for which I was thankful.

In the village I lodged in a house belonging to the headman. He said he first came here in 1956 to marry the old chief's daughter and stayed on, though normally the bride goes to live at the groom's home. The village had a population of 540. Zafimaniry people were different from plateau folk in that they were not originally a rice culture, living self-sufficiently on beans, maize and fruits. But nowadays the ubiquitous rice had taken over and its cultivation had escalated the soil erosion.

The village was set in the fork of a stream, the neat rows of huts squashed on to this rare flat piece of land, with occasional huts on promontories down the valley. The huts were made of upright wooden planks lightly decorated by chiselmarks, and roofed with slatted bamboo hooked over the ridgepole and held flat with bark ropes.

But the special feature of these huts was the intricately carved wooden doors and window shutters, chiselled with fan-shaped patterns, or linear, or circular whirls. Wood carving had been a custom here since the days of the Kingdoms, but the carvers' skills were not discovered by foreigners until 1965 when famine hit the area with an invasion of rats from the east which devastated their maize and bean crops. In order to survive a Jesuit priest helped them gather and sell their carvings. When the villagers saw how well they sold, they carved with such zeal that the hardwoods in the forests regressed almost overnight. It is not thought that their work has any ancient religious meaning, beyond a certain warding off of evil by the carved doors. It is purely decorative – art for art's sake. As I wandered round the village I noticed a couple of houses' gable ends were topped by carved birds in flight. The granaries were small storerooms on tall stilts with hefty rat preventers. I watched maize being pounded by young women and timber being sawn by young men, while infant boys played with carved spinning tops, lashing them faster and faster with a bamboo rod and fibre rope. The best performers could crack the lash under the top to make it jump.

Hats were worn by young and old, reed-plaited square pillboxes without a brim, a bit like a Catholic biretta. Some girls had an elaborate hairstyle of eight plaits each side woven into a butterfly bow, and threaded through itself which was quite a work of art, though not dissimilar to how they wove their grass mats.

Coming back to my lodging, I walked in through a carved front door but found myself in the wrong house. The occupants were somewhat surprised, as I backed out with many '*azafady*' (sorry, excuse me). But it was an easy mistake to make and I frequently had trouble remembering which house I was staying in.

Inside, the hut was eye-stingingly smoky, and, whenever I opened a wooden window, many children's faces peered in. My host had some wood-carving work to do. Having sawn a new trunk into planks, he was marking these with chisel lines, tapping along with a chock of wood as a mallet. The chisel was so old it had practically worn to a stump. His wife was heating a cauldron of newly harvested rice; since they have no ground which is dry enough or flat enough to use as a drying place, they have to dry the grains slowly over the fire.

The hearth was set in a patch of earth in the floor, with three stones to hold the pots. The rest of the floor area had grass mats on wooden floorboards and, near the door a slatted low wall made a handy chicken coop. I negotiated the price of a chicken to supplement my supplies for Silberb and Co who continually whined that they were hungry. They were being unhelpful, taking me to meet people whose greeting was 'Give me money'.

Silberb egged them on, 'Give this boy a present, give this woman your shirt.' I pointed out that I hardly carried presents for 500 people, but my comments fell on deaf ears. Other people brought sick children to me asking for treatment and medicines. When people invited me into their houses it was only to harangue me with their demands or to try to force me to buy uninspired artefacts: an incised wooden box, a wooden honey jar, and a double-bladed bayonet type of knife set, the two blades each slotting into the other's handle.

In one hut I met a woodcarver whose daughter-in-law had just produced her first baby. She was sitting inside a matting tent raised over the bed, like a square cupboard, which afforded a minimal sort of privacy from the in-laws. The bride price was as little as 400–5,000 fmg, then worth £2, now worth half that, but in this village it was still considered a large expense.

I heard that tour operators had started to bring groups of tourists who give the villagers whatever they ask for. This accounted for the behaviour of Silberb and Co, who tried my patience to the limit and I lost my temper when they demanded I buy them rum. I realised I had to go beyond this place before I would find the real Zafimaniry.

Feeling cross I went for a walk. Being in the fork of a stream, there was water gushing through several parts of the village with ample natural stepping stones to cross it. A stroll required recrossing the stream several times. Going south I came to a junction of paths with a curious assembly of standing stones on a tomb-like pyramid. I was being closely followed by a troop of forty little girls at the time and when I stopped they all bumped into the back of my legs. On second examination it was not a tomb, its centre held a large stalked mushroom of stone enclosed by thin slabs of standing stone probably representing memorials to individuals or families. A line of stones can symbolise each corpse in a communal grave which I remembered had to lie out of linear sight of the village.

The stones were covered in mosses and ferns, and at the front was a lip of flat stone where I sat facing a view of descending mountain ridges in drizzling cloud. Here against the east escarpment it rains 250 days a year.

The noise of rice being pounded and sifted beside my open door woke me before dawn. It was full bodied work, hips and shoulders moved in a slow whiplash motion with every heavy pounding stroke. People passing the open door called 'Salaama', not the 'Manaoahaona' greeting of the plateau. Clouds began engulfing the village, which helped when I went out for nature's calls, as not one hut in the village had a long-drop or any form of loo.

The give-me give-me money demands started up after breakfast; several people demanded my trousers and my shirt, it was as if their one purpose in life was to strip me bare before I left. I added the chicken to Silberb's load and refused to let him kill it since while it was alive it would keep longer. The lads' appetites were full of worms.

I couldn't wait to leave that village and hoped our twenty-kilometre walk would be far enough to bring me to some real Zafimaniry. The climb to the ridge took less than an hour, with elemental clouds rushing up and over us, and through the jumble of crags.

The lads were in a surly mood and I was in a rage with them. Their whining had led me to an outburst of temper and I now felt a little nervous of the consequences. I had to tell myself to calm down and be careful, from their narrow-eyed expressions it wouldn't really surprise me if they attacked and robbed me on those slippery paths.

At a single log bridge eight metres long with a flattened surface that had somehow become skewed at an angle, I was halfway across when, instead of waiting, Silberb and Co both jumped on to it together and made it bounce appallingly. I concentrated on my balance and hurried across.

So I did much of the day's walk alone, lagging behind just enough to keep them in sight, and catching up occasionally. At midday we caught sight of Antetezandrotra village, nestled on a low hill ahead, with neat square rows of huts and a Catholic church surrounded by wild roses and white trumpet-flower bushes in full glory.

As I paused to admire this pleasing view, I was overtaken by some people on their way to the village. One was a barefoot Catholic priest, aged about sixty, who seemed to skip along. He lifted my spirits and invited me to lunch when I reached the village.

Lunch with Père Hercule Courau was a great pleasure. His eyes were bright and his mind still youthful, though he had lived here and to the north-east for twenty-five years. Now he was doing one of his monthly ten-day walks around his parish, about which he cared passionately.

He explained how the Zafimaniry traditional diet of beans and maize, grown by slash and burn agriculture, had formerly given the forest enough time to regenerate after farming. Even in colonial days, while many other regions were replanted, there was never an attempt to reafforest this remote area. 'In 1970 there were still many trees here,' he said, waving his walking stick at the denuded hills as far as the eye could see. 'But where there were twenty huts there are now eighty.' This he put down to the decline in infant mortality. 'Nowadays men have to make week-long treks to find fine hardwood palisander trees, even smallish ones, and the palisander is dying out because the seedlings need the shelter of a micro-climate where big trees break up the force of the rain. And, sadly,' the father continued, 'since the forest has gone, so have many of the plants that grew beneath it, which means the loss of traditional medicines, and without the medicines you lose the knowledge of healing.' It was a depressing picture.

Beeswax, another forest product, used to be a valuable resource, and Père Courau explained how he organised the collection of beeswax for sale abroad as furniture polish. Honey had been an important part of the local diet. But because the forest no longer has enough fodder for them, the number of bees had dwindled. People still kept a few hives in the forest, but nowadays men had started stealing the honey from these. I asked what punishment a thief is given if caught.

'It's no big offence to take honey, but if an outsider is caught stealing zebu or pig, the villagers may kill him. The problem is, if you let the thief go he'll come back with twenty or thirty friends and set fire to the house or village which caught him. So either you have to allow him to steal your livestock, or kill him, or face the revenge.'

It seemed a hard choice for a godfearing man. I changed the subject. Père Courau of course knew all about the standing stones, known as *vatolahy*, many of which represented memorials where the dead body of the person commemorated was never found. 'A child I knew drowned in a flash flood during the cyclone, and the river took her body so far we never found it; the family decided to put a standing stone for her.'

Without a standing stone, you can have no funerary rites, which is possibly the worst fate that can befall a Malagasy. No burial, no ceremony, means the soul will have a painful and restless existence unable to gain entry to the ancestor world. It causes the death of the soul. The erection of the stone is a means of reuniting the family in death, giving physical reality to the memory where the bones are not present.

Père Courau told me the village's tombs were in caves in the rock. 'If you take this path uphill you'll pass in front of a cave tomb that is now full. Lots of them are full and recently this village had to start a new tomb. When that happens you have to shift a few of the ancestral corpses to the new tomb to establish which families have the right to use it.' He described the long meetings that had to be held to decide exactly which ancestors to move. They took five in the end – it had to be an odd number – and this also left five spaces for future use in the old tomb. To all Malagasy the rights to family tombs are crucial. If you let a corpse in, its offspring and future generations have burial rights in your tomb for eternity. In some regions the wife is buried in her husband's tomb, in other places her body returns to the tomb of her father, having been only on loan to the husband. Children usually belong to the father's tomb but various exceptions make each case the decision of the Chef du Tombeau.

'You can lose your rights to the tomb if you break *fady* too often, or if you are judged to be a witch. Witches who have done little evil may be allowed in but their heads lie to the south. A child born on an inauspicious day who gets killed or comes to a bad end may be barred, as are uncircumcised males. Specific diseases can also bar your entry, or if you marry outside your social class. To be barred from your tomb is the ultimate disgrace; the greatest punishment a person can undergo. It dooms you to being forgotten for ever, and because it is like a sentence to hell it's rarely administered except for serous crimes against the community.'

I asked the priest what were his hopes for the region, and here he paused. It was hard to know what to hope for in this isolated area which had never seen a vehicle. He seemed to have reconciled himself to the infiltration of traditional religion into his Catholic teaching and, in the end, his answer was a practical one. 'Maybe if people kept more domestic livestock, if they made an effort this year, they could avoid famine next year. There's a widow woman in a village near here with a population of 400 who began raising chickens and she's now the richest woman in the place. She's a good example for getting on, but no one has followed her example. People here don't seem to follow examples. Another local widow had seven children, and now she has more zebu than anyone. She had managed to bring up her family by producing local goods to fit needs, selling chickens, potatoes, whatever people asked to buy.'

Our lunch was simple fare of chicken and rice and tea. Then I took my leave as the father had work to do and went to find Silberb. In the village my lads were installed in the headman's house and I met his eldest son Jean-Baptiste who worked as a teacher at the local school, though by nature in all his spare hours after classes and at weekends he was a woodcarver. He tapped away at the diamond-shaped detail of a wooden chest as we talked, and I sat on a gorgeous carved bench he had made when he was twenty.

He learned to carve from his father when he was fifteen, and now his young son was already playing at carving.

He consulted his seventy-five-year-old father between my questions and told me the village was brought here by his grandfather in 1928 because their original village was cursed. People in every family had fallen ill and many youths had died in their teens. There was no obvious cause of death, Jean-Baptiste told me, and so they consulted the *ombiasy*. The sorcerer said if they stayed in the village they would continue to die. He said someone had buried a poison in the village to kill the young men.

I asked more about native poisons, the source of which appeared to be ready to hand in insects and plants, and freely used before the advent of Christianity. Poisons could be made from scorpions, spiders like the grey Matahora whose name means 'fear', various beetles and hornets, or the water insect Tsingala which kills cattle that swallow it when drinking. Among the plant poisons are the nettle-hairs of the Agy bush, the poisoned thorns of the vine Avaotra, and other lethal roots, berries and types of bark. There was a time when guilt or innocence was decided by a judicial administering of poison. The favourite was one concocted from the tangena bush which, if the accused died, it showed he was guilty. If he lived he was not guilty. Perhaps an acceleration of heart rate due to fear on the part of the guilty could have something to do with the poison's quick action.

The wood-carving school teacher explained how a properly made fetish poison includes not just the physical poison but the plant or insect's evil desire to murder. His father was twelve years old when the elders had decided to move the village. The old man remembered coming here and showed me the hill where his father had chosen to build their new house. 'It was dense forest here in those days,' he said, 'so we cut space. And when the village was established the health of our people improved. And people multiplied.'

While packing up I offered some crumbs to our chicken. The lads said it wouldn't eat bread because it had never tasted it. They were right. It pecked the bread once then left it alone. Shame the poor doomed bird didn't eat its last banquet.

The most dramatically positioned village I visited was Faliarivo, perched on a craggy outcrop above a cliff. The huts were tucked in among even-sized boulders, somehow still making tidy lines of carved doors. The kids played with spinning tops of a wood ball on a metal spike, curling a string round the spike and hurling it at the ground to spin on its point. Young girls played hopscotch using an eight-square configuration; you have to hop on one foot while kicking a piece of wood on to the square ahead of you.

I stayed with a lady of dubious repute. She had three small children but Silberb assured me she was not married. Her house was a one-room affair full of fleas but I was getting used to them. There's a Malagasy saying 'to be as undecided as a flea between two mats'.

I was making a conscious effort to get along better with my lads and I thought they were trying too, but they still didn't give up demanding gifts. *Cadeaux* was one French word they didn't forget. And their other maddening trick was to exaggerate the distances ahead, attempting to make a day's march out of a two-hour walk.

In the evening I lit some sparklers for the children, and made end-of-line friends with a dying man. Old age had caught up with him and his time was over. I'd gone into his hut by mistake, as usual, and didn't like to leave too hastily. He said people spend their lives trying to keep death at bay and safeguard themselves against its ultimately irresistible power.

But every rule said 'not this way', he observed. It was always a prohibition. No *fady* (taboo) says '*Do* this'. Life was like a war against things that threatened to break up home and happiness, health and prosperity, which, if not guarded and secured against, could lead to ruin. To live in accord with the *fady*, from the womb to the grave, was not easy.

At morning assembly time I made my way to the primary school. One hundred and forty pupils were split into two classes but one of the classrooms had fallen down in Cyclone Geralda, and there was only one teacher. Assembly involved neat lines, an arm's length apart, and full-throated singing of the national anthem. The older class had a maths exam with blackboard questions like: If one square metre gives 4 kilos of beans, what is the total weight of beans in a field measuring x by x. Rather them than me.

I went walkabout on to neighbouring crags and could see the second class dancing in a circle holding hands in a ring-of-roses-type game around the biggest bunch of standing stones while they waited for their next lesson. Down below some older girls who had left school were guarding the rice paddies against raids by birds.

Watery sunshine, drizzle and low clouds were in continual movement. Some farmers passed me on their way to seventy-degree sloped plots of sweet potatoes, the men carried blades and spades, some worn down to the butt. The spade, most basic of tools, had its own set of taboos and must never be left in a field at night in case it got poisoned. When resting it should never lie flat like a dead man, and when carried it should not be allowed to flash in the sunlight. And, in the rules of seniority, elders should not carry spades if their younger brother or son is with them to do so.

Knowing that I'd had enough of Silberb and Co, I changed our route and programme to get rid of them as soon as possible, ideally that day if we could get back to Amtoetra where the jalopy-road ran out. We took a route along a ridge of granite no wider than the path. It was spectacular, like a great saw of rock with us going up and down along the granite teeth, but we were rewarded with brilliant views to several villages until we crested on to the plateau which was very boggy.

By now I was barefoot and found it preferable on the many unstable log bridges; some floating log walkways were more lethal than useful since they swung sideways under my weight, while the marsh grasses in the streams threatened to sink bottomlessly beneath my feet. But I like the way that bare feet puts one in touch with the ground and one can tell immediately what is slippery or unstable. Streams were fresh and cold while marsh water was warm and oozing.

Farmers carrying headloads of sweet potato leaves (like spinach) and baskets of ginger roots hurried past me on the path as we approached Amtoetra. Tomorrow being market day they would exchange their wares for salt, paraffin and candles, and when I heard the flute music in the breeze I knew we were back.

On market day I hoped to find a lift to the main road, and then to my delight I learned that Père Courau's vehicle was due in to collect him and the local harvest of beeswax. At dawn I was woken by a man delivering a ten-kilo plug of wax, and others soon arrived with four kilos, seven kilos and a mega twelve-kilo plug. While waiting I looked in the church. Its altar was a thick slab of stone two metres long, which had taken twenty men several days to carry from a distant hill. Everyone praised Père Courau for his dedication, even the women at market were grateful to him for chipping footholds in paths and improving bridges so they could safely bring their produce to market. I knew I had met a saint of sorts.

7

As the moon waned the celebration of Alahamady, the Malagasy New Year approached. On the eve of the new moon I linked up with my girlfriend Freddie again in Tana and we went to the sacred royal hill of Amboimanga where we became part of a vast crowd thronging an ancient stone slab lane. Despite the midday sun the sunken lane was mossy and cool, shaded by leafy trees. The whole hill is covered with trees which are protected as this has been a sacred place since the beginning of the nineteenth century when Amboimanga became the ritual centre of a united kingdom of Madagascar.

I couldn't understand why it wasn't raining, it had rained every other day. But the astrologers had predicted no rain for the two-day duration of the festival and it was they who announced the chosen days, at the coincidence of new moon and a Friday, since all that begins on Friday goes well.

The brightly dressed crowd streamed up the hill in high spirits. Food-stalls along the lane were selling bananas, rice-cakes, noodle dishes and yoghurt. The lane climbed for another long kilometre.

Finally we mounted a flight of old stone steps and entered the great open ceremonial area in front of the walls of the queen's summer palace. Accordion music, rattles and a bongo-style drum jigged out a fast rhythm and made the mood lively.

The centre of attention were two zebu due for sacrifice the following morning. A wrinkled woman with a trident was pushing back the crowd from the bulls. By now Freddie and I were in the thick of the surging mob, allowing ourselves to be pushed by the eddies and counter-eddies like a tidal flow in a rocky inlet. We were trying to avoid being pushed out on to the great flat sacrificial rock, stained with old blood and bits of withered intestine.

On the upper terrace stood the current King of the Sakalava tribe and some elders, and speeches were being made. Freddie told me that the most senior man present was sure to be the most toothless one.

'There's the King of the Betsileo,' said Freddie pointing to a white-bearded man with a white ceremonial *lamba* round his shoulders. 'He lives south of here near Fianarantsoa which is an ancient centre of literature and learning. Most of the kings are still recognised as kings but they don't live in palaces and have no political power. When I had some business to do in the north I had to inform the king, out of respect for him.'

The King of the Betsileo made the next speech while holding up a long thin pipe-pumpkin with sacred water in it. 'The water in that pumpkin can heal sick people. If you drink just a few drops of it you will be miraculously cured,' whispered Freddie.

'To find out which king will hold it in the ceremony a spirit manifests itself to one of the kings in his dreams, and the spirit appoints the chosen king.' Freddie's tone turned dubious, 'Any king could say he had the dream, couldn't he?'

Although she was a shy young woman, Freddie was being a superb help by translating what was happening and if she did not know about a custom she asked the people around us, using my presence as an excuse. In fact a great many of the city-folk had no idea what was going on, and a woman attendant was sent to instruct the crowd to remember the *fady* that forbade the bringing of alcohol or umbrellas and the one about removing their shoes. Shoes are *fady* because they signify superiority. The ancestors' seniority comes with age not wealth. It used to be *fady* for a man to wear shoes if his father had none. Another woman attendant was marking the foreheads of certain individuals with a white chalky substance.

This ceremony had not been held for a hundred years, the last time was in 1895, and now it had become part of a move to bring tradition back to those who had lost touch with their roots. It acknowledged the modern world's need of the past. Perhaps the island's increasing economical problems were because the ancestors were displeased. There were even some who went so far as to suggest that the ancestors had caused Cyclone Geralda because they were feeling neglected.

The invocation of the ancestors began with the words of the time-old formula and sacred water in pottery urns being ritually offered in front of the bulls. Musicians worked with gusto on drum, rattle and accordion. Guards in red headbands and red and white *lambas*, carrying three-pronged spears, lined up beside the bulls which swung restlessly towards the crowd. As one we recoiled, somewhat frantically as the bulls tangled in their ropes. A guard sorted these, while the red bull kicked out and tossed its horns.

The second bull was red and white with a white blaze and white legs with regular brown splotches. These were sacred markings which meant it would automatically belong to the royal family, regardless of the original owner. As Freddie explained, 'When you have something like that which is so great, you cannot own it, you may only be its guardian. We have a proverb which says "You can never possess that which is priceless." This rare bull is sacrificed to gain the love of our last king, asking him to look after us. It represents religious power; the red bull represents political power.'

The bulls were now securely tethered each by one back leg to a tree's roots that trailed solidly down the terrace wall and made rich mossy patterns on the stone.

The invocation of the spirits of the ancestors was followed by music to conduct them back into this world. A man in front of us went into a trance, trembling and shaking his limbs, head lolling and eyes closed, possessed by a spirit animated by the music, and other spirits began to manifest themselves in people all around us.

One girl with thick black hair was throwing her head and torso from side to side, jerking with frenzied spasms. An attendant tied a red scarf round her head and the crowd cleared a space in case she fell. After five minutes she collapsed in a heap on the ground and her scarf was taken to put on someone else. The scarf is to protect dancers in a trance. Without the scarf, I was told, they could vomit blood and die.

Suddenly individuals were pushing their way through the packed but friendly crowd, like mad fishes wriggling through waterweed to reach the open space where they danced into a trance. The music whirled, whistled and whooped, whipping up the crowd.

The woolly-haired girl revived, still in a trance, put a pot of sacred water on her head and danced on. The pot was seized by a man who sprayed water on her and doused her hair, then she flicked her head in every direction showering everyone around.

Only the person in the trance and some of the elders know which spirit has possessed a particular dancer. But people said Rakotmadit was the spirit who had taken the girl. He had been a favoured soldier of a Sakalava king.

'What are these spirits?' I asked.

'They're *zanahary*, messengers,' answered Freddie, 'spirits that can communicate. When the spirit is in you, you are a slave to it. During the trance it will talk through you and people can ask you their private requests, like how shall I pass my exams? The spirits have to tell the truth.'

As soon as someone was fully in a trance the women attendants hurried up to try and ask for messages, and Freddie said, 'Only the person in a trance can understand what the spirit is saying. Suppose someone has done something very wrong, he can ask the trance slave what he can do to obtain forgiveness, and the slave has to ask the *zanahary*. You can't choose your *zanahary*, you have to deal with the one that takes you over. It's different from Christianity in that you can't make a direct approach to the supreme being. You can't speak to him unless you go through the ancestors.' She was logical about the ancestors. 'Dead people are closer to God, they know more about what is right and wrong, so the living must listen and learn from the dead people.'

Freddie sneaked away to whisper her secret request to the attendant. I teased her about it since she still said she didn't understand the ceremony or the traditions involved, but she was interested in finding out. She said there was no answer yet because the answer had to be relayed by someone in a trance. I did not press her to tell me what she had asked. I recognise the taboo and, having had many wishes in my life, I know they can only be answered if they remain genuinely secret, kept like a seed in the dark waiting for the right time to grow into existence. Later I spotted Freddie trying to send her question again and she nearly succeeded: a girl with entranced eyes turned up to the sky was talking to an attendant.

'What's she saying?' I asked Freddie.

'She says,' Freddie paused for a moment with a perplexed look, then translated enigmatically, 'The spirit said it had nothing to tell us, but it was having a good time.'

I asked a girl we got talking to if she had ever been in a trance, but she giggled and said that she would be afraid. Freddie explained, 'It would be all right at an event like this. But if a spirit just decided to manifest itself in me whenever it liked, when I was at the office, say, I'd be scared of it, too.

'Just think of carrying a spirit around inside you that can come out when it likes, and you have no control. Each time you hear lots of music it could manifest itself. How embarrassing.' She was also nervous today because the trance spirit could make its host person point out someone else for it to go into. So no one was safe from its power. The idea of Freddie dressed in her finance house suit tapping away at figures and reports, and suddenly being taken over by spirits and trances was indeed to be avoided.

This day was a preparation for the morrow, and the crowd was swelling continually. There were now about a thousand people present and a wonderfully dramatic atmosphere. The ritual washing of the bulls began in utter silence, then the accordion started while a couple of children were selected to walk forward and throw sacred water over the bulls. Afterwards many people took turns to splash them with sacred water, but respectfully. They were not being baited. A man stood before the bulls and told them to be calm, which was difficult for them when it came to lassoing their legs to tether them for the night. The red bull was fighting and kicking fiercely.

Beside me Freddie was marked in chalk on her forehead to reinforce her wish. At dusk there were more trances and people dancing in the midst of the crowd. But most of the trances now were not the genuine article, contagious excitement leading to wild displays which failed to find the upper levels of communication. No alcohol meant no drunks and, despite the huge crowd, there was a superb atmosphere of kindly togetherness. Women were singing, lightning flashed, but without rain.

A procession formed in a semi-circle round the bulls, with candles in coloured paper lanterns. Drums began to beat and the vast crowd clapped rhythmically.

An orgy was scheduled for the night, when all sexual taboos were allowed, even supposed to be broken, particularly those *fady* concerning cross-caste sex.

It was time for us to leave.

By eight a.m. the following morning I was back with the crowd, an orderly mix of families from the villages and townies out from Tana, now swelled to about two thousand, in front of Amboimanga's palace. In contrast to the unrestrained build-up of the eve, New Year's Day celebrations began with a Christian hymn, and praying hands, beseeching God's presence on this heathen day, followed by somewhat blasphemous amens. On stage a man swung a goose over his head, offering it to ancestors north and south. Someone marked my forehead with chalk. He said the mark was the same as on the zebu's forehead, and it was a mark of special welcome. A procession of women approached, their heads laden with sacred water, bananas, bottles of pale brown honey, sweets, a plate of white clay balls; one round-faced handmaiden had thick-rimmed owl glasses below her fat pottery urn.

A build-up of anticipation rippled through the crowd. Spearsmen kept the numbers back and the guards with tridents lined up once more in front of the bulls. The goose was still being tossed to and fro above us at the top sacrificial stone but a moment later its neck was wrung. The bulls would be killed at the big lower stone.

'Who drinks the blood?' I asked. 'Not me!' said my companions. Today I was with an eminent group of new friends, UN dignitaries and Malagasy nobles from the capital. The nobles on the upper terrace this morning included descendents of various royal families and some men from Reunion Island whose ancestors had been nobles here. They all knew each other and their genealogies, since nobles are not as numerous as Hova (freemen) and they have intermarried among themselves for generations.

The action was just below them where guards wearing red headbands untied the red bull first and two men grabbed a rope trailing from its back leg, pulling it to the ground. More men hurried to secure the red ropes. Everyone wore something red which is the royal colour and a symbol of power. They held the bull down on the ground and freed the ropes from its horns; their hands, faces and backs were by now covered in white chalk. Eight men held the tethers on its legs, one man on its horns. Another rope was attached and it was thoroughly trussed up, every leg and horn tied together and front legs tied to back legs.

An attendant offered to lead me up on to the top platform and, once there, I edged to a niche on the brink of the parapet by the smaller sacrificial stone. This put me just above where the bull was lying. We watched a slightly gory sacrifice with blunt spears, and waited for a sign that God was with the people. The Chef de Cérémonie danced crouched under a sheet with a large red heart embroidered on it, representing God's love.

President Zafy arrived to signify government support for the traditional side of Malagasy culture, and a few people grumbled because he stood on the old king's favourite spot.

The Chef de Cérémonie under the sheet took an urn of sacred water and offered it aloft to the bulls. Sacred water comes from a particular spring on the hill, explained Jean-Claude, a former government minister who was born nearby and used to collect water with his grandfather for household use from sources on the same hill. In the old days there was a private source for the king or queen, and their bath was filled with water carried by virgins.

'Myself as a boy, I was made to draw water at four or five a.m., before the first bird flew across the stream because that is when water is at its most pure.'

The chef flicked some of the water on to the zebu and then he went along flicking water on the heads of the head-loaded ladies. Musicians struck up a fast tempo. The dead bull was sprawled on the stone; the other waited its turn; people were selected to be marked with chalk dots, and an old man wearing trade beads and a blood-splattered white robe was rubbing his finger in blood and marking people with a red line from forehead back into their hair. His other hand held aloft a ceremonial blade decorated in geometrical motifs. People hurried around with spears and empty buckets amid a sea of bodies dancing with hands fluttering and waving in the air.

Beside me an elder stepped up on to the small sacrificial stone. I thought maybe he wanted a better view, but he bowed his head and closed his eyes. A man carrying a full bucket of blood stopped in front of him, lifted the bucket and emptied it all over the elder's head. He seemed to be pleased.

He was the Chef de Palais and was taken in procession to stand in front of President Zafy. Would they pour a bucket over him too? The procession walked off round to the back of the palace.

'Everything today should be directed and carried to the palace, as a sign of respect,' explained a Ministry of Culture friend. 'The zebu are the path to the palace and the carriers and all servers carry the blood as a sign.'

Blood drinking had started by the bull's body, with quick handfuls scooped out of its jugular by the bodyguards. Various important people were given marks of blood smeared on their faces and hair. Then much of the crowd rushed up to be marked on face, head and tongue. One brought a jamjar for takeaway blood.

The surviving royal bull started pulling restlessly at his tethers. By now there was no blood left in the first one. Suddenly the royal bull's knots came loose and he walked into the crowd, his ropes trailing behind him. Two people grabbed a back leg-rope but couldn't halt him. They were jerked forward by his strength. When they pulled back, they only succeeded in angering the bull who charged at them. The inevitable happened. They dropped the ropes and ran, the bull turned and lowered his head to charge at the crowd. People all around grabbed the loose ropes, fighting to control the kicking beast until he was brought down.

After this second sacrifice someone reached down inside the bull to find its heart and liver, then both carcasses were flayed open by men who sharpened their knives vigorously on the stone. A man with a cup filled it from the beast's chest and drank it; all protein, I thought. Another, with a huge smile, managed to get his plate right inside the carcass.

Plastic cups and jars were being passed forward.

'Why are they taking the blood?' I asked a man with a knife.

'To put on your own head. You can take it and do it at home, if you prefer.' I looked around for Freddie. She needed to get a jar for her prayers. 'Can I take it for a friend?' He gave me a congealed blob which I wrapped in leaky foil. Then I met a royal descendent. His mother was one of the children of the king's sister. I asked if I would be allowed to make a prayer. He couldn't anoint me since he was of royal blood but he showed me someone who could and said this year there was much to pray for. Near me someone launched into a shopping list of prayers saying, 'My house has fallen down, my wife is sick, someone has stolen my land, and I need money.'

I found Freddie and told her where to go and get anointed and, suddenly self-conscious, she insisted I went with her. 'Ask this chap,' I pushed Freddie forward and she talked to him, then he anointed her while making the ritual speech of blessing. Whether or not the people believed their prayers could be answered, they could do no harm, and revealed the naive Malagasy optimism combined with resignation which makes them a nation of dreamers.

Freddie admitted that she found Christianity confusing, with the different practices of Catholics and Protestants, but as a Malagasy she was in no doubt about certain things. 'Before we do anything important we have to consult our ancestors, and before I came to Europe I went to my family tomb to let them know and ask their blessing. I prayed that I could achieve what I was supposed to do, then come safely back to Madagascar.'

Although there are still recognised kings in other regions, the Merina are not allowed to have a king. Their right was abolished by the French colonial forces who fought their way to control of Madagascar at the end of the nineteenth century. The royals kept their heads low for safety and over the ensuing generations of independence and socialist government policies they continued to forget their royal lineage.

Later on in Tana I had lunch with Alain Ravoaja and André Ravelonanosy of the Merina royal family who told me, 'Up until the end of socialism no one talked about having royal blood. Princes can now acknowledge their ancestry but the king is still a banned role. The king of the Merina would be the most powerful man in Madagascar. He could claim to be king of all Madagascar following Radama I who had conquered and united most of the island by 1825.'

I asked André how he grew up and he remembered his grandmother telling him, 'When your grandfather's brother Prince Ratrimoarivony married the last queen, your great-aunt Princess

Rapeliasinoro was first in line to the throne. The Prime Minister Rainilaiarivony was an ambitious Hova who wanted to marry every queen. The second queen he married was the adoptive mother of that princess. So after the queen's death your great-aunt refused the crown saying, "I don't want to be the wife of the husband of my mother." ' I agreed it sounded complicated.

Rainilaiarivony accepted her refusal and looked elsewhere, deciding to marry instead the wife of Prince Ratrimoarivony, but first he had to kill the prince. André's grandmother said the Prime Minister called the prince to his palace and told him he looked ill. 'Not at all,' said the prince but the Prime Minister insisted on sending round his personal doctor. The doctor gave the prince poison, he died, the Prime Minister married the widow, queen number three, and put her on the throne.

In fairness to him I had heard that he was a very capable prime minister who governed well and did much to modernise the state. The noble lines seemed to me to be pushing brotherhood into endogamy. My two friends at lunch were related to each other on both sides of their family. 'We are brothers-in-law and we are cousins,' they explained helpfully. I thought how intertwined the royal family tree must look. But I learnt that a few years ago André had begun some research into the various lineages with a claim to the throne, knowing that he had royal blood from both his mother and father's lines. His mother was Zanak-andriana which is the royal class and highest caste of aristocracy, making him a royal prince, and on his father's side he was Zazamarolahy which also made him a prince, if a slightly less grand one. Being the eldest, he realised that he himself was probably the head of the royal family.

Now a local regional president, he enjoyed his duties. 'I want to help people, to work for their wellbeing. The people need help. But I don't want them to depend on me, just to love me, as I love them.'

THREE

Lemurs and Lightning-Making

8

One of Madagascar's downsides is that few things work. At the house in Tana the phone was dead as usual, most frustrating for all the urgent calls. But somehow the things which are so important one moment stop mattering when you can't do anything about them. That morning the coffee percolator failed on me, so I strained the coffee through a cloth, murky and grainy.

All this made me happy to get back on the road, enjoying packing my rucksack, and this time putting in my old inflatable canoe. It rolls up ingeniously no bulkier than a tent. The paddles divide into four short parts with connectors. It all went into my not-very-big backpack along with small tent, sleeping bag, cookpots and some gifts; everything I should need for a few self-contained weeks.

I was muzzy from a late party, quite a party, extravagantly thrown at the Carousel, the ranch of an exclusive riding club, to welcome teams of riders from neighbouring countries for an international jumping competition. The South African team spoke no French and one member was so afraid of the food she was living on bread. Which was her loss for the banquet was Malagasy haute cuisine with delicacies like thrice-fried beef, shredded like seaweed, excellent, and vine-leaf wrapped meatballs. It was yet more impressive since their cooking-gas had run out, their stockist had none, so they had cooked a feast for a hundred people entirely on charcoal. Their phone didn't work either, the copper wires were always being stolen from the poles to refurbish the table-football games, a popular roadside attraction.

The South Africans were a novelty in Madagascar. Until the ending of apartheid they would have been refused visas. Now they were busy discovering the island's opportunities. A rumour which intrigued me was that another group of them were planning to bring over a hundred racehorses to invest in the sport and rebuild the racetrack. The horses were said to be fully trained Thoroughbreds, and after the racing season would be used to breed and upgrade the local stock. Great news for the racing scene. I wondered if they would arrive in time to solve my problem for this season's races.

We danced until three a.m. The guests of honour didn't realise that the party could not finish until they had left, they thought it would be rude to go, and I couldn't leave since the host had the only car and had to wait for the party's end. In the end I told the team to say good night myself. After all, their jumping competition would be taking place in only a matter of hours' time.

Having packed my bag in the dawn hours I was at the taxi brousse station by seven a.m. heading for Fianarantsoa. Normally there is a nightmare of clamouring porters and taxi ticket sellers, but the instant I arrived I heard a voice 'Christina, I wondered if we'd meet again!'

It was Fanja, whose name means a bud of peach blossom, a young woman I had met in London when she had decided to run away from her crooked English husband. Her home was in Fiana, she was going back to reunite with her long-lost family, and there was one space left in her taxi brousse. For the homecoming she was accompanied by two charming brothers to help with her massive suitcases. The route to Fiana was memory lane for her. I enjoyed watching her reactions, and we talked endlessly over the next eight hours of taxi brousse travel with its inevitable breakdowns and overheatings. For me it was also memory lane, having driven the road with my future husband when we were courting.

Fanja's excitement mounted as we entered town and I enjoyed being there at her homecoming, her brothers staggering under her luggage, as we walked up the old steps of the hill and started searching for an aunt who had moved house. The town is built on three levels, the sprawling lower town straddling a small river, the 'new town' built in grid pattern by French colonials, and the ancient upper town where we traipsed along misty cobbled alleys. We passed several churches and went up another paved stairway, my companions calling out 'We used to live in this house,' and 'Remember that one?' They pointed to a gorgeous rickety mansion.

We found the right house eventually, and a delightful aunt whose first words were, 'Don't cry, don't cry.' Later, gales of laughter came from the earthen kitchen where one brother, who was a chef in a Chinese restaurant, was organising our dinner. I sat in the living-room leafing through the family photo albums. Aunt Volola had been a beauty, married but divorced because she bore no children. Fanja's mother was dead and her father had remarried and lost interest in his children. Fanja's own marriage had been a disaster, her husband seemed a petty and brutal type who liked to make people fear him, and when Fanja realised he was wanted by the police she ran away. She confessed how her heart beat at night after she escaped, fearing he would find and kill her. In Fiana she was safe, with two big strong brothers.

She and I shared the spare double bed, though she was hardly in it since Fanja and her aunt stayed up talking into the early hours. The mattress was stuffed with something hard, probably chopped straw. Feathers are not used for bedding or pillows in Madagascar because feathers symbolise flight; they threaten the security of the home and are therefore *fady*. Fanja had flown but she had come home.

I spent the next day wandering through Fianarantsoa as moral support for Fanja. It was tough for her continually being asked where are your children and your husband when the answers are none and gone. But we found a favourite uncle who lived at the base of the hill with a stream running beside his house. Fanja exclaimed that used to be a big river, but the uncle replied, no you used to be a small girl. Her cousins, his three daughters, had grown up and were all studying at law college and there was again much merry chatter when they arrived to find Fanja there. For all that, Fanja was a little wary of submerging herself in family life and losing her newly won independence. I told her she could find me in Ranomafana next week if she needed a break from her dutiful role.

My travels would take me down to the south-east coast where I planned to use my canoe which was still tightly stowed and took up half my backpack. But first I wanted to see the rainforest and its wildlife.

*   *   *

Ranomafana National Park spreads nearly forty thousand hec-
tares up Madagascar's eastern escarpment at a height of between
400 and 1,600 metres. The trees were lush with ferns, fungi, mosses
and orchids. The river pouring down beside the village was clear
and bubbly with cascades, and on the way to the park entrance you
walk past the biggest waterfall in the country. My backpack was
reduced to basic camping food and mini-tent; and I was striding
strongly along the road towards the park when a taxi brousse from
Fianarantsoa direction lurched to a halt and out jumped Fanja.

'I'm coming, too,' she announced cheerfully. I eyed her tight
jeans dubiously and the small holdall containing her make-up
pouch. She had brought nothing for camping and no food, but
was sure she would have more fun than staying at home. I had
also collected a local research guide, to see me on my way,
so the three of us set off into the forest heading for a hilltop
clearing promisingly called Bellevue.

The way was immediately steeply hilly and tightly folded, the
forest a secondary tangle with a sunny top to the canopy. Down
below were wispy vines, bamboo lianas and thin trees, all using
each other to support their passage upwards in corkscrews, or
clinging, inexorably squeezing into and strangling their hosts. It
takes five to ten years for a strangler vine to kill a host tree and
by the time this has died and rotted away the strangler has become
strong enough to stand alone. Seeing all this profusion of plants
crowded together, reminded me of the thoughtful poet Armand
who we had met in Alarobia on our calèche journey and his verses
on the social needs of plants. Here they were demonstrated all
around me. I could see that plants need each other, to live with
or on like the vines, or to shade each other, or for pollination, or
to feed each other by putting nitrogen back into the earth like the
legumes. They compete for space and struggle for survival when
everything starts to grow. They also protect their young, sheltering
them with their leaves from the storms' force. Some must have
shade until they are adult, and their seedlings use their leaf litter
as compost. During winter all the leaves fall and decompose to
nourish the seedlings. They have long-term relationships with their
animal and insect partners too, like the butterflies and birds they
aim to attract through their looks and behaviour. And some seek

to start up new colonies, with seeds whose burrs attach to passing people and animals or travel more privately by first being eaten.

Some inveterate travellers latched on to our ankles – leeches. I stopped to pull off a couple. 'Oh my God,' squealed Fanja when she looked at her feet covered in blood. The blood carries on flowing for some time because the leeches use an anticoagulant.

In a forest clearing we put up my tent, made camp, collected firewood and water, and brewed up a dehydrated expedition supper. Fanja said that every day after I'd left, her aunt mentioned me during grace before meal times: 'And please God don't forget Christina, she is far from home, please look after her and keep her safe.' I wondered if Fanja missed her aunt's cooking as well as her praying.

Fanja admitted to being hyper-scared because she had never been out at night in a forest, and never camped in her life. At that moment a striped civet fossa came along the path. He seemed quite untroubled by the light of my torch and it held him in its beam as he sniffed around for food. Fossa are the largest carnivore, after the crocodile, in Madagascar, and are extraordinary because one type can climb trees, yet looks like a small dog; another can't climb, and the biggest type, the Ranguku is like a small panther. This latter is rare but stories persist of babies whose mothers put them down on the ground for a moment, being dragged away by the fossa when their mother's back is turned. Generally people only fear the giant fossa at night, or by day if it is disturbed.

A full moon had risen. A second fossa came along. In the tree trunk beside me a mouse lemur was joined by his friends, and another pair of red eyes on a tree trunk turned out to be a 'nocturnal gargoyle', a type of gecko that hunts insects and small frogs. A small tree snake got caught in the beam of torchlight and Fanja said to leave it alone. Fanja is a Betsileo and she explained, 'We believe dead people's spirits can be transformed into snakes. So snakes are sacred because of the spirits. If it has certain wrinkles or perhaps a scar we may recognise a dead relative, and after any funeral if you see a snake in the forest on your way home, you let it pass quietly.'

The night was damp and it rained. Thank God for the sheet of plastic we'd tied over the mosquito tent. With the two of us squashed in a one-person space I didn't like to turn over in case Fanja woke and was too alarmed for further sleep. But at one point I did get up to rescue some fruit when I heard something pass by munching. I had left our unwashed plates and pan outside and found they had been licked spotlessly clean.

At dawn I listened to birdsong of ringing falling notes, then a trilling song and much general chirping. I liked the way the sounds hung for a moment in the stillness under the forest canopy. For the major dawn chorus, there were a hundred species of choristers here including Paradise Flycatchers and various shrikes, also tree frogs, new species of which had been recently found in Ranomafana.

I walked to the nearby forest clearing named Bellevue for the ranges of hills you can see all around. Clouds were starting to lift out of the valleys, outlining the trees. The first rays of sun warmed me through after a night on the damp earth. Brown lemurs were also sunning themselves, one leaning back with its hands clasped behind its head against a branch. More lemurs came along flicking their tails and leaping past through the trees en route to their feeding grounds.

As I walked back to camp I encountered two lemur Rubriventer, which live in pairs and have one infant a year. Males are differentiated by white half moons under their eyes. We were also likely to see the lemur Varecia Variegata, a three-kilo black and white ruffed type, eating fruit and spreading its seeds through the forest. The largest of the twelve lemur species in the park is Milne-Edwards' Sifaka, a six-kilo heavyweight that lives in family groups of between three and nine members and eats leaves, fruits and flowers.

Our second day's trek took us into primary forest with its canopy at ten to fifteen metres, with enough light for layer upon layer of lower vegetation, lianas, tree ferns, and bushes inhabited by small creatures. Now we were noticing some massive tree trunks and I could see why people are so keen for the park project to succeed in preventing the area becoming deforested.

Eco-tourism is the buzzword. The twenty-eight villages surrounding the park are being assisted to improve their standard of living and decrease their dependency on slash and burn agriculture and on the forest hardwoods. Sustainable use means leaving

A calèche a long way from home, and being tested in the wake of Cyclone Geralda, above; below, our guide Roland with Edouard and the calèche team.

Above, a village in the Zafimaniry wood-carving region and, below left, an example of decorative shutterwork. Below right, typical architecture of Tana, the island's capital.

Above, Tana, the city set among twelve sacred hills; below left and right, Tana's vast and famous open-air market.

Above, bed and breakfast Malagasy-style in Ranomafana in the south-east; below, children's games with the rice delivery cart in Ranomafana.

Alahamady, the Malagasy New Year festival, is celebrated at Amboimanga. Above, two royal generations, survivors of the many historical kingdoms, who hold respect but no political power today; below left and right, blood from the sacrificial zebu and other domestic offerings are taken to lay before the ancestors.

Above, a two-masted schooner, not unlike those used by the pirates who haunted the south-east coast in the seventeenth and eighteenth centuries; below, travellers' palm stands out elegantly in the abundant forests of eastern Madagascar.

Memorials to the dead on an island obsessed with the rituals of death and continuity of life with the ancestors. Above, standing stones, zebu horns and a Christian cross; below left, *aloalo* in a Mahafaly graveyard, carved with scenes from the life of the departed; below right, a Christian mission graveyard on Isle Ste Marie.

Above left, heading into the sacred gorge on the Manambolo river; above right, baobabs, the upside-down-tree that is said to live for ever; below a crocodile siesta spot provides a campsite on the Manambolo.

something for future generations. Of course the motivation is not just the survival of the local population, it is also to try and secure a genetic plant bank which will serve all mankind. When our modern farming is hit by crop disease, we now seek out disease-resistant original forms of those plants. It is vital for us to keep the gene bank topped up by places like Madagascar which are so rich in variety of unique plant life. To try and lessen the slash and burn, the project researchers are using technology to improve the rice paddy fields. The aim is to integrate conservation with rural development, and keep the local people at the centre of the action, so that they would co-operate and not feel excluded.

The Duke University in South Carolina, USA, was supporting the researchers. After trekking up and down steep hills for many hours we found the two-tent camp of Deborah Dogosto, a field zoologist who was willing to tell me about her work.

She and a colleague first came here to study a particular lemur called Hapelemur Silus, which was described as a large-sized grey bamboo lemur. They thought they had tracked one down but it was gold, not grey, which was puzzling. Over the next few days they had several good looks at it and realised this was something quite different, a completely new species.

A couple of weeks later she saw a grey Hapelemur Silus which was grey but had white ear tufts sticking up which made it distinctive from the usual all-grey bamboo lemurs. 'So this was three types of bamboo lemur in one area, and that's rather a special thing, since very few mammals live on bamboo.'

There was plenty of bamboo in this part of Ranomafana, I noticed, big clumps of it. Deborah went on to explain how the different species of lemur eat different parts of different bamboos, so they don't compete with each other. Her new gold lemur feeds on the pith and outer layer of the tips of tall bamboo. 'When we tested it with chemical analysis we found it contained a lot of cyanide. If you or I ate as much cyanide for body weight, we would die after every meal. But somehow these animals either pass it through their system or don't digest it.'

I asked Deborah what she had been working on that day and she told me they were clearing and marking old trails that had not been used for a while. Some hikers had got lost recently for three days before they were missed and a search party was raised. 'I've never been lost. Sometimes I'm not sure where I am, but I know all the local ridges, so I only have to climb up on to one to work out where I am.'

Deborah would stay camped here in the forest for several months writing her doctorate on two groups of lemur, the brown Fulvis Rufus and the red-bellied Rubriventer, similar yet with very different social systems. Red-bellies live in much smaller groups, and her study was to see if this was accounted for by their different diets.

The amount of food available is the factor controlling the size of the groups. After one stint of eleven months' surveillance, Deborah's brown lemurs disappeared from the study site. After six weeks they came back. 'At this time of year there is obviously no fruit in this patch of forest, so they go down to the lowland slopes and the guava groves. They range a surprising distance of seven or eight kilometres; they are not big animals, that's a long way. All this tells us how big an area you need to maintain each species.

'They move around in daylight and also at night, which is mysterious, so sometimes at night we go following them. It's not easy to follow a cat-like animal, eight metres up in the trees, through the dark and the mud and the leeches. When the animals stop you doze in the rain and cold for a couple of hours, then find they've slipped away and moved off.

'The leeches, I guess I've gotten used to them. I had a colleague here one year and we had contests every day. One time I had sixty on one ankle.'

It was nearly dusk when we parted from Deborah. 'My favourite time of day is now,' she said, 'and at this time of year when the sun's low a lot of animals get active. You'll see all my groups when you go up the first ridge.' I was pleased that our paths had crossed. As we trekked on, the guide told us another new lemur was rumoured to exist but it had not yet been caught or recorded. 'None of us has seen it yet, no scientist that is, but the villagers tell us it's there. It's either a new species or a sub-species.'

Madagascar is famous for its forty odd species of lemurs and a primatologist and palaeontologist called Jonah Ratsimbazafy who became a good friend told me he had found sub-fossilised bones of now-extinct giant lemurs up north. There used to be several gorilla-sized types, a sloth-like lemur with very long arms, and a cow-faced lemur larger than a man. There are no monkeys in Madagascar because the island split from Africa before they evolved. And that's why the lemurs have diversified to fill the roles of other animals and birds.

The main differences between monkeys and lemurs is that monkeys are cleverer, lemurs are more primitive and more gentle. The latter have a wet nose designed for sniffing and smelling things out like cats and dogs, while monkeys have a dry nose like humans because they use their brains not their noses.

One evening I sat trying to lure a group of shy lemurs over to share a banana. None would come near except a youngster who plucked up enough courage to snatch and run. He carried the banana back to the group and began eating. I was surprised no older lemur took it away. Finally one of the females took it. Lemurs are female-dominant. Apes and monkeys are male-dominant.

Jonah was also studying lemur behaviour and had recently been surveying three groups of stripy-tailed catta lemur. In one group a baby lemur was orphaned, he clung to his dead mother for the whole night wailing in distress. The next day a young male went and took care of the baby, and the day after his aunt took care of the orphan. She already had a baby but she also allowed the orphan to suckle too, only occasionally pushing him roughly away, and carrying both babies on her back. A month later the aunt's own baby died, and she kept the orphan until it matured.

Life in camp in Ranomafana involved damp firewood and cold baths in mountain streams. Fanja and I found a pretty one with a deep pool to lie in, but it was extremely cold. After drying in hot sun I felt so good I went back for more. The best moments were spent just sitting quietly, especially where the territories of different animals bordered each other. Lemurs patrolling their boundaries chorused their territory calls in rivalry. Sometimes there was so much hurrying hither and thither I felt I was sitting in a central bus terminal for lemurs.

Jumping between trees the red lemurs made horizontal leaps, unlike sikafas which leap with vertical posture in the air. I watched a fulvis miscalculate his leap. He grabbed for a branch, missed, and fell through the twigs below, clutching at them as they broke. He hit the ground in a moist leafy spot and bounded away unhurt.

I began to distinguish the infants' lost call. The fulvis made throaty cooing noises and the young red-bellies went quissht, quissht to attract their mothers. Among adults there is also a set of contact calls, like 'Come here I've found food', which is a set of clucking grunts quite different from their territorial chorus.

When a ring-tailed mongoose came along the trail the lemurs retreated. The mongoose eats almost anything including small lemurs, as well as lizards, snakes, worms, eggs, and it goes swimming to hunt fish and frogs. The other highly curious mammal I saw was a tenrec, a spiny little thing between a shrew and a hedgehog. This one was striped yellow and black lengthways. Its quills are barbed and, when angry, it raises a bristling neck ruff of quills, and hisses and rattles; the rattling comes from its mid-back quills vibrating rapidly. Quite a noise for a tiny creature. To communicate with their family group they use high-frequency quill vibrations, inaudible by humans. Some tenrecs also make clicking noises, which may be some animal radar.

The most arduous walk we had was at the end of our stay, doing a six-hour hike against time. It was three p.m. when we set out on the return leg, and we were racing to cover what we could of the steep boggy mountains before darkness overtook us and left us stumbling around in the night. We hardly stopped to pull off the leeches. Fanja was a star, she didn't have the strength to walk fast but she made herself do it; and faster as darkness came closer. We saw a big wild pig near our path, and we watched each other cautiously.

There was little twilight, we rushed through the end of day and into the start of night. It was nine p.m. by the time we reached Ranomafan.

At the hotel the head guide had spent his wages on a bottle of rum and became heatedly argumentative about the park's right to be there. Rural development had not made them rich. He claimed that only the foreign scientists and researchers were benefiting from the place. If the locals could hunt and chop trees in the park, their lives would be improved. He ranted on about how ten years ago they had plenty of everything, life was good and they sacrificed zebu every month, but now they could hardly afford it once a year.

Of course he would not know the whole world has become poorer in the last ten years. I tried to explain the global recession but he refused to abandon his high expectations. When I suggested he was drunk he said in a rather Betsileo way that he wasn't drunk but the rum was too strong.

Over a late supper Fanja confessed she had done rural development work some years ago during her military service. She had been employed in a campaign against illiteracy. 'I was sent to teach villagers to read and write, to give them the chance to learn to count, so that they could take their agricultural produce to market without being cheated. And reading means you can read a letter of family news if one arrives.

'At first I was so afraid of these people, because I was only nineteen and my students were old people. During training I was not afraid but when I walked alone to my area I wondered what I'd do if the people told me to go away. Maybe they would think I was just showing off my education. Maybe no one would come to the class.

'As the days passed I discovered that some of my students lived three, five and seven kilometres away, and it surprised me to see people walk so far to listen to me. At first I took my own lunch to the village or just bought some fruit, but when they saw me eat alone the villagers decided that each day I must eat at a different house. In this way no one had the whole task of feeding me and I got to know who lived in each house. It was an important experience for me and I learned as much as my students did.

'Some of the development teachers in other areas were afraid to eat village food in case it was poisoned or the villagers had used black magic on it. But I decided I had to trust people. If you show them you don't trust them, they'll never trust you.

'A couple of my colleagues caught fever and died. Their parents said they died of black magic because the villagers had not liked them. I wanted to help people to like me by showing them that I was no different from them, so I wore their type of clothes, sometimes walking the five kilometres to the village barefoot.

'At rice harvest time I didn't want to tell them to come to classes, they had far too much work, but nor did I want to abandon them. If I'd stayed away from the village during harvest they would not bother to come back afterwards. So I walked there every day to help with the harvesting. When it was all gathered in we went back to the classroom.

'For eight months I worked in that village, and I learned to have confidence in myself, and to realise that I don't need to be afraid of people.'

While in Ranomafana Fanja and I visited the very rundown Hotel Thermale and hot springs, badly hit by the river in flood during Cyclone Geralda. The hotel was a simple colonial-style place with guest bungalows, all currently empty but for fleas, and gardens with paths and fountains and flowering bushes.

The wrecked footbridge we had to cross to reach the hot springs made Fanja dig in her toes and refuse to try it. I had to coax her across step by step up the twisted planking. At the higher mid-section most of the planks were loose or missing, and the handrails were long gone, wrapped around trees downriver. Fanja clung to my arm in barely suppressed panic but I admired her nerve.

Hot water from the source used to fill a swimming pool on the riverbank but this was now cracked and empty. We found where a hot spring came out of the ground, and dammed the stream with wood and stones to make a deeper pool. We looked forward to enjoying the result of our labours but when we tried to get into the pool the water was so hot Fanja made noises like a scalded cat.

Adjusting our dam to enlarge the pool cooled the water enough to lie in. There's something blissful about tired muscles in hot water. Above us some yellow sunflower bushes were in full flower, which Fanja said meant winter was here, and poinsettia was in red leaf, having changed dramatically from creamy-white through pink to scarlet over a month.

The next day Fanja went back up the road to her family in Fiana and made me promise to stay with them again on my return trip in a couple of weeks' time.

9

I found a lift to the coast with a bunch of schoolchildren who had been competing in Fiana's provincial school games. Beside me was a fifteen-year-old girl long-jump champion who could jump 4.13 metres. The perky victorious mood evaporated along the rutted road as our 404 wagon collected more and more passengers until it bulged. We were twenty-five in the back. I couldn't even raise a hand to scratch my nose. Every traveller to Madagascar has a horror story of a taxi brousse. It seemed *fady* to complain and when I yelped at a mother and baby sitting on top of me, there were frowns. No one else grumbled at the crowding, no one said there was no more room. Perhaps because when they waited by the road, they knew that space would be found. For those hanging on to the tailgate outside, it was raining hard. Local people walked about under banana-leaf umbrellas.

At Mananjary I booked into a small hotel in the colonial-style town, functional more than prosperous, in an area growing vanilla, pepper and coffee. Its fate had changed for the worse with a rebellion against French colonialism, after the Second World War. Extremists were egged on by the movement for Independence, and during the rebellion many French and pro-French Malagasy were murdered here. It had also been an excuse for people to take revenge on their Merina overlords.

The son of Mananjary's District Officer at the time had lost eight of his family in the massacre. An estimated ninety thousand had died during the rebellion, many from starvation and exposure because they fled the French troops but didn't know how to survive in the forest. Then Mananjary became a backwater.

It is here that the Pangalanes Canals connect a chain of lakes and lagoons, for freight of local produce. My interest in Mananjary was partly because I had been given a not very hot clue to a stash

of treasure, which I found by chance years ago in a book about
Madagascar in the Royal Geographical Society Library. I didn't
take it seriously but since I was here I resolved to keep my eyes
open. It had potential because it was in a very old book in French
and perhaps no one had looked at it for decades. There are books
in the RGS Library that go back to the early eighteenth century,
and since my French is fluent I had tackled this one for some
research on the island coasts. The page was covered in scribbled
notes and dates of ships and values, all meaningless, except for
the cryptic note 'Mananjary – search where the sound of the
ocean is muffled.' Idly diverted, I tucked a copy in my file of
'things to do in Madagascar'.

The most famous Indian Ocean treasure map was auctioned by
Christie's some years ago, it purported to show the location of
riches beyond one's wildest dreams, but although various people
have tried, none has ever succeeded in finding it. Pirates in the
seventeenth and eighteenth centuries used the coast of eastern
Madagascar as their base for attacks on shipping in the Indian
Ocean and the Arabian Sea. My other interest in this watery area
was the chance to use my inflatable canoe again. The Pangalanes
Canals seemed a good place to test it out, check it for leaks and
start relearning to be steady in it. As I remembered from last time
I took it travelling, it could wobble dreadfully. I didn't intend to
get wet.

The waterfront around the pirogue park and market place was
too public as a starting point, so I followed a village path towards
the main arm of a canal. Two footbridges out of town there were
fewer people about, just farmers going to the market. But in the
twenty minutes it took me to inflate the canoe and assemble the
paddle, the bridge became crowded with onlookers who insisted
on helping me into the canoe and tendering assorted advice. So
I set off into the Pangalanes canal system paddling smoothly
into the breeze on a broad waterway between banks of reeds,
bullrushes with cigar heads, water hyacinth in flower, wild yams,
palm trees and tall casuarina. Along the way I passed occasional
huts where fishermen worked with hoop nets. One of them pulled
up a bunch of sunken reeds and shook what it harboured into his
sack. Elsewhere women in pirogues were setting long nets.

My canoe ran aground several times but the worst element was the rain which frequently poured down from a black stormy sky. Once when no shelter was available, I pulled the canoe on to a sandbank and propped it up on driftwood to improvise a roof while the worst of the weather passed over. In the next storm I met an old man who told me that in his youth the Pangalanes were busy waterways used by canoes carrying up to eight tons of fruit and vegetables to colonial markets. As I knew, the island was quite late on the colonial scene, not thought worth colonising and apart from efforts to establish footholds there by the Dutch, Portuguese, French and British, it was widely by-passed en route to India and the spice islands. Ultimately British and French interests grew in rivalry and in 1890 they signed a treaty whereby Britain relinquished Madagascar to the French in return for the French giving the British the island of Zanzibar. It was not until 1896 that France established control of Madagascar.

Then as now the waterways were the communication arteries. There was never any road access to the cultivated patches along the river's upper reaches, so people loaded their harvests on to bamboo rafts and punted downriver. I saw several of them, wedge-shaped rafts with a small low shack of thatched palm leaf where the boatman sleep. They live on the rafts while they sell their produce, then sell the raft as well and return home on foot rather than have to punt back upstream. One of the raftmen eyed my precarious craft and told me to be careful at sea, since mightier things than my canoe have been sunk by the unpredictable and violent storms. There are indeed many sunken and wrecked boats in these coastal waters; wrecks old and new, the most recent being sent down by Cyclone Geralda. The older types were East Indiamen, heavy merchant galleons and tall three-masted schooners, some reputed to be carrying treasure. He told me that fishermen sometimes found gold cups and coins washed up on the beach. One man found a chest full of silver coins.

Silver coins were the currency of early Madagascar, obtained by trade with the outside world. The country could not then, as now with foreign exchange, acquire enough coins for its needs, so they cut them into pieces, their value being calculated by weight.

Uncut coins were so precious they were given to the ancestors at festivals.

The clue 'muffled sound' could mean the treasure I had read about lay underwater, and undoubtedly there was much at the bottom of the sea here. But my previous experience of scuba diving on sunken wrecks had left me cautious. My main memories were of the strangeness of swimming down ladders, seeing cabins tilted sideways or upsidedown and covered in sea ferns and barnacles, with only your breathing to disturb it, and the bubbles to tell you which way is up.

After I had bid the raftsman goodbye and was alone again on the creek, a distant roaring of water made me think of a weir or rapids but I knew there were none here. I paddled curiously on. An hour later as I rounded a bend I found I had taken a wrong turn; I'd come into a river mouth opening into the ocean, with rollers breaking and surging up the river. I made my way carefully along, among big canoes with square sails that ferried passengers and cargo across the estuary. These were Antambahoaka people who have a mysterious sacred site up the coast that looks like a sculpted white elephant. It was meant to be the work of some descendants of Mohammed who landed north of here and passed through leaving the white elephant behind.

Not to push my luck I was heading for a side channel but, rounding the point, my craft was broadside to the waves, which slapped at the canoe and tried to roll it over. I thought of the many shipwreck stories I had read about this coast. Various sailors managed to reach the shore. One Robert Drury who was shipwrecked off Madagascar in 1701 was an educated youngster of fifteen, whose father had been sending him to India with trade wares. He spent the next sixteen years as a slave to the Antandroy royal family, working with cattle, eventually becoming the royal butcher. He married, and was promoted to ritual butchery, a position of some importance. During a local war he escaped across the desert to St Augustine Bay where ships from England were known to call. But he was out of luck, and recaptured to be enslaved this time by a Sakalava. When Drury heard that another ship had come in he wrote a note on a leaf and tried to smuggle it out to the captain. But his messenger lost the leaf and put another one in its place not realising its significance. So Drury spent a couple more years on the coast where he was treated well enough. Finally he was allowed to leave for England in 1717. The end of his story is certainly a cautionary one, for he later returned to Madagascar as a slave trader, making use of his personal experience.

This treacherous coast, however, was no place to be musing on history. I steered hard left after a sandspit and caught an eddy that helped me upstream, then floated me down. Later beside a sandy beach near the ocean, I thought I was in calm water, until I realised there were waves breaking just beside me, invisible from my level except for glimpses of spume and spray as they curled and broke. People do not swim in the sea here, it is too steep and full of sharks. Unlike on Madagascar's west coast where the coral reefs keep the sharks offshore and provide them with plenty of food, so they are not aggressive, the east coast sharks are hungry. For fishermen, death by shark is not uncommon. Equally common for sharks is death by fisherman; their fins have a ready market among the Chinese, and the meat is eaten locally.

I saw a hammerhead glide to the bottom beneath the canoe, it was small and wriggled into the sand. With those great sideways hammer lobes on its head it didn't look as if it could get much of a bite on things. The streamlined ones frighten me more; the grey sharks I met once while scuba diving were the same size as me. Several began circling me and before long there were twenty of them. I had been instructed not to panic unless they arched their backs.

Sometimes the shark had the last laugh. Nearly a hundred people had died a couple of months earlier in a neighbouring town from eating poisoned shark. No one managed to identify the poison, or how their meat might have been contaminated with toxic algae. The forty-bed hospital received nearly four hundred patients, but fortunately the epidemic had now finished.

This coast is also known as the Whale Highway, it is the first land the migrating Humpbacks see after leaving Antarctica. They spend the summer feeding in Antarctica, since cold water is rich in plankton, and come up here to breed just up the coast beside Isle Sainte Marie. Whales don't feed much when they are breeding and, contrary to what one thinks, warm water is poor in plankton, so they leave as soon as the baby whales are large enough to make the journey.

In one creek I found a beauty spot of bamboo, palm trees, mangoes, tulip trees, and a type of smooth elephant ear, the leaves growing on short stumps that gave wonderful reflections on the glassy water. There's something ingenious about the way that plant grows, rising from underneath the water. The seeds are dropped as the waterlevel reaches its minimum and after germinating in the mud they grow rapidly to stay above the rising watermark. Like banana trees the elephant ear base trunks are formed of old foliage, and the leaves are often cut for wrapping things.

Some of the villagers I saw occasionally on the banks were wearing clothes woven from raffia: one woman had a raffia skirt and several men were wearing jackets woven from it, and waistcoats and T-shaped shirts. I doubted the clothes were very washable, and they did look rather like old sacks. I talked to one group, asking if they too had heard of pirate treasure. After all, it was recorded that there had been nearly a thousand pirates living on this coast in their heyday and if they were all stashing treasure some of it would surely come to light. They agreed that bits did appear now and then, but if they knew any more they weren't letting on. Some of the local people are known to be descended from pirate ancestors who intermarried with the local population in the seventeenth and eighteenth centuries. The pirate cemetery at Isle Sainte Marie has gravestones going back to 1788, and I found one appropriately engraved with skull and crossbones. In the eighteenth century the son of an English pirate became king under the name of Ratsimilaho, ruling part of this east coast.

By now, however, I was cold, wet, tired and hungry. Treasure trove could wait for another day. Two young girls approached me as I wandered along the beach in this resigned mood. They said they were so poor, would I please buy some precious stones they had found. This was not a pirate legacy, there are mines for precious and semi-precious stones dotted throughout the country. These were uncut red tourmaline, amethyst, beryl, emerald and sapphires. I bought their two sapphires, which was the closest I would get to buried treasure on this journey. But it would not have surprised me if they were old Vick glass jar fragments washed smooth by the ocean. One day I would make the effort to find out. Treasure trove is not always what it seems.

10

I was now heading for a mysterious region around Vohipeno further down the south-east coast, the mystery being that no one could tell me much about it, apart from the fact it was the source of some sacred books and an old Arab tribe called the Antaimoro. They had once been important in Madagascar, but no one could remember why. To get there I went south for a full day quite comfortably, having hitched a lift with a Ministry of Health car, and reached the town after dark. It boasted no hotel as such, but there were a couple of Malagasy *hotely*, the first had a rum-drinking party going on but the second was fine, except for the slippery garbage heap they escorted me across to reach the rooms. Speaking only Malagasy, they gave me the room on the end, £1 a night, and a bucket of water and scoop, and a second small bucket whose purpose I already knew. I hung my food supplies from a string in the hope of outwitting the geckos, and sent out word that I needed to find someone who could speak French to be my guide.

A young lad called Paulin arrived later in the evening. He said he raised chickens and used to have a hundred until a few years ago when he neglected them and they died. Now he had started again with twenty chickens and a male turkey, saving for a female.

The word turkey, *vorontsiloza*, means 'bird which is not unlucky', and there are no taboos about keeping them, but it is *fady* for young people to keep geese because young people have 'green hair' (youth). Only grey-haired people may keep geese, their colour countering the forces of the grey geese.

Next morning Paulin and I set off on foot to visit the king of the local Antaimoro region and in the five-kilometre walk beside the River Matitanana I could see it was an area prosperous with coffee, cloves, peppers and bananas. Local fruits included avocados, lychees and mandarins. I could tell which fruit was in season by the peel scattered on the track, and the smell of an orange being eaten quite far away. We clanked along, Paulin carrying a couple of bottles of rum that are the obligatory gift for the king's retinue.

It is not known whether the forebears of the Antaimoro people came from Arabia, Egypt, Ethiopia, Yemen or Mecca. The most likely theory is that they were an Arab tribe who fled from the Arabian Peninsula in the fourteenth century because they didn't want to submit to Islam. They had some Muslim ways but they also had their own customs which they refused to discard. The militant Muslim leaders ordered their massacre and they were chased southwards. The only survivors escaped to sea in great canoes and the ocean currents took them towards Madagascar where they settled.

The fugitives brought their knowledge of medicine and surgery, their books and their customs of sacrificing zebu and worshipping the stars and idols. They wore the *djellaba* and had primitive gunpowder weapons. Of the people we met along the way, some men still favoured Muslim-style robes and the women wore the fez-like four-cornered Antaimoro hat. The lost tribe arrived into a land that was sparsely peopled. There was plenty of room for more. The local population marvelled at their medicine and writing, and treated them like gods.

As time passed, the local people brought their sick to be cured by the Arabs, and consulted them on many matters, eventually welcoming some of them to live in their villages as doctor-cum-priest. The Arabs found this role so demanding they had no time to cultivate food, so the peasants looked after their fields for them. By the next generation the Arabs were ordering the villagers around to suit their own whim; they had married and multiplied in the villages, creating small Arab, now Antaimoro, communities alongside the original villages.

The Antaimoro have retained hereditary kings for about four hundred years. There also used to be small kings ruling several villages as vassals to the big kings who made sure villages under any one vassal formed a patchwork, so nobody controlled an entire region.

When we talked about local customs Paulin said the most important one for the young men was the circumcision ceremony that only happens once every seven years.

'We slaughter an ox and the feast goes on for several days. We all dance, and every day more boys are circumcised in public by various skilful elders, and then they become men. Boys long to be circumcised. Their friends tease those who are not and make them ashamed. You tell your parents that if they don't get you cut, you no longer want to be their son.'

Fady has a lot to do with this. Uncircumcised boys are not permitted to eat legs of chicken, which are reserved for men, nor wear a hat, nor handle sharp iron instruments. This latter at least seems sensible for children, though the logical extension is a bit extreme. Because you are not allowed to cut an uncircumcised infant boy's fingernails with metal, the mother must bite his nails short with her teeth. Until you are circumcised you are not of course allowed to marry. And if you die, you do not have the right to be laid in the family tomb.

The ancestors have to attend this ceremony to prevent accidental bleeding complications, to stop any squabbling between the participants, and keep things correct. The prayers are in Arabic and with the songs and felicitations, they stress the importance of sexual fertility and procreation. In fact almost the whole of Madagascar practises circumcision as a fertility rite. It is an order from the ancestors.

We arrived at the king's palace, a big hut raised on stilts around three central posts. The posts were set in place centuries ago and successive kings periodically replaced the wood and the travellers'-palm walls and roof. We took our shoes off before entering, made a presentation of the rum, and sat on floormats near the king.

Quite a young man, the king drank no rum himself, but shared it out among his numerous advisers sitting cross-legged on floormats. He seemed affable, knowing his role meant he had to accept visitors such as myself. Though few outsiders visit the region, those who come would all be expected to stop and pay their respects to the king. Perhaps because I am a woman, at first he only wanted to speak through his committee, but in fact his French was better than theirs and when he got fed up with correcting them, he spoke for himself. He also had a *katibo*, a scribe, who was in charge of the holy scriptures that the original Arabs had brought with them. These scriptures are called Sorabé, from *sora* meaning holy writing and *bé*, big. The Sorabé can no longer be deciphered by Arabs, it has changed so greatly over the passage of time, the words being Malagasy and the script being ancient Arabic.

The Sorabé books are sacred since they contain all that belonged to the tribe's ancestors, their customs, history, legends, scholarship, divination, geomancy, and useful tips on how to walk on water, be invisible and throw lightning.

Writing had a significant power over illiterate tribes. It seemed supernatural and the *katibo* who 'performed' it owned a force. Before battles, they sent their enemies things like miniature coffins covered in inscriptions which struck terror into their hearts. Not having seen writing before, they succumbed to its magic, and knew they were beaten. Writing gave the Antaimoro power and prestige throughout Madagascar. In Tana King Andrianampoinimerina (that's the short version of his name) encouraged them to set up a school, the first in Madagascar, in the early nineteenth century. They intermarried with the royal family and were influential in developing a system for the administration of the expanding kingdom.

The Antaimoro still make their own writing paper from the bark of the Avouha tree which they boil and reduce to a paste, dry, reboil, then spread it to dry like parchment. The pen is made out of a very rare bamboo living only deep in the forest. They soak it in a special fluid then dry it, sharpen it, soak and dry it again and resharpen it until satisfied with the point. The ink they invented long ago turns yellow after many years but cannot be erased, a fact demonstrated in books a hundred years old. Some sacred books were ten centimetres thick. If you want to look at them you must respect Islamic law and abstain from pork and alcohol. In each generation several apprentice *katibo* are still trained to maintain the tradition, learning by copying out the oldest manuscripts. Every seven years they update their history.

Antaimoro writing was the only script of Madagascar until the first missionaries brought the Roman alphabet. After the Second World War sadly many of the books were collected and burned by over zealous missionaries. The Catholics called the books diabolic sorcery and destroyed all they could find. The Protestants were also guilty, though they kept some of the books out of the fire.

Before becoming king of the Antaimoro my host had been a schoolteacher. He became king after his father's death. Though when a Malagasy king dies one does not say he is dead, one says that he has run out of life, or he is lying with his back to the people. The circumlocution for commoners is to say they are 'broken' or 'lost', and the dead person is 'he who will never be seen again'. Among the Bara clan, the dead are called 'Rafanjava' which means Master Shining, and is also the name of the moon.

The attendants have to hide the corpse while all the king's subjects assemble, then they announce the death. The king must be buried in the night, and during the same night his successor must be crowned.

The schoolteacher had been a reluctant king. Though he had always known he would become king one day he had enjoyed his work in a primary school. I asked if the two jobs were rather similar, but he did not laugh. He said that when he heard he had become king he felt a heavy weight descend on his shoulders, and knew he would never be free of it. These Malagasy kings seem to take the office seriously.

The schoolteacher's response reminded me of a prince of a neighbouring people, I had once met. The moment his father died he had run away to the north and refused to come back to assist at the burial. For a Malagasy, that was scandalous enough behaviour to prevent him becoming king, so he stayed free.

The schoolteacher king tried to do the job: 'I discovered quite early on that you can't solve all the disputes or judge things right all the time, and everyone criticises your mistakes. That is why I have a big committee of advisers, to share the blame.' The advisers didn't look worried, they were going hard at the rum.

I was taken to visit the royal burial ground. These were 'houses', not graves, sited in the village and only divided from the living by a flimsy fence. We went to a gateway where I was told to put my shoes *on* and take off my hat. How different, I thought, from the plateau where we had to be sure to go barefoot and there were complex *fady* to keep the dead separated from their villages.

Then the *katibo* spoke the ancient Arabic rubric before opening the gate.

The 'houses' contained long trenches beneath the floor for group burial according to status. A new cadaver has to be laid beneath the others so that his impure fluids of decomposition do not fall on the older bones, a respectful if highly inconvenient arrangement. Personal effects of the deceased were laid out in the house of the dead in the same places they would have occupied in the house of the living. Several of the dead houses were guarded by wooden human effigies now extremely old, and all that remains of the missionaries' cultural demolition job. Each house also had a standing stone beside it which seemed to be designed to break the lines of *vintana* or destiny emanating from the dead, to prevent them having a bad effect on the village. At one particularly large standing stone I asked how many men would have carried it to this spot and my companions explained it had flown here in ancient times. It had flown a hundred kilometres to land here at the request of the *katibo*. Such powers were not thought magical, they were metaphysical and the instructions for wielding them were detailed in the Sorabé for those capable of learning.

Walking around the dead houses had made us impure and Paulin insisted we wash our feet and hands in the river. This was the river I intended to canoe on the next day.

In search of information about the possible dangers of the river I went to meet a friend of the king, the Catholic priest Père Vincent who had twenty years' experience of this area. I guessed he must be quite elderly, but it was impossible to tell from his strong face and clear commanding voice. As he spoke, he hunched forward, radiating interest and concern for every detail of what surrounded us. He said the river's upper reaches are stiff with huge crocodiles, and where the river squeezes between rocks is where the crocs like to lie and sunbathe. Every year someone gets eaten by them.

Père Vincent was not at odds with the *katibo*, they had long ago recognised his dedication and goodness. 'One day they came to me with their witnesses and asked me what my real name was and my date of birth. These were such unusual questions I asked why they wanted to know and they said they were doing their seven yearly update of the Sorabé and they wanted to take the opportunity to include me and my work in their sacred book.'

The father's work was with handicapped children and at the mission the older ones were taught a trade. I was able to visit the remedial centre for the younger children next day as I took my canoe upriver. Children scampered about wearing metal braces on their thin legs and in a hall the sister introduced me to a crowd of three- to four-year-olds doing physiotherapy exercises. Some had their legs strapped flat to tables to help strengthen their spines while they did sit-ups, the advanced ones held heavy bags of sand, others stood upright bending their withered knees and raising themselves upright, again holding sandbags. Shoes could be built up to equalise the length of legs with local rubber and bamboo, but the metal for the calipers was heavy; not the lightweight aluminium we use.

The centre came about because twenty years ago when Père Vincent was new to this region he was told there was a devil-possessed child in a village. 'Take me there,' he had said. He found a handicapped child with epileptic fits, and knew then that his work would be to alleviate such suffering. Twelve years ago he built the centre which now treated about seventy children. Solar panels provided energy to run the fridges, lights and hot-water treatments. His practical solution for suffering and his dedication are something I have long admired in the Catholic mission field.

With final warnings from the mission about crocodiles, and much waving from the children, I returned to the river. I was below the rapid section, where the valley became broad with a lazy current, and I paddled idly, watching the ever-changing perspectives of grassy hills as I rounded each bend.

The river is considered sacred and when an Antaimoro returns home after an absence, he makes a point of coming to the river where he scoops up handfuls of water and pours them over his head. Every seven years the Antaimoro go to the riverbank where their ancestors first landed and make offerings. It is said that one of their kings died during that first voyage but they kept his body and buried it near the river. Trees overhung the bank and where possible, cultivation reached right down to the water's edge, taking advantage of the fresh silt from the dropping riverlevel to produce groves of grapefruit, oranges, mandarins, avocado, lychee and breadfruit. Père Vincent had also told me that one of the mysteries of the area was the petrified fruits which were occasionally dug out of the ground.

'It was just here by the river,' he said, 'when a bulldozer was making the road to these villages, we started finding prehistoric fruits.

'One evening a lad came to the mission bringing an avocado which seemed to be made of stone, almost like brick and of reddish colour. I marvelled at his ability to copy nature but the lad insisted that it was God who made it, not him, and that he had found it on the ground by the river.

'The child gave me the fruit and I rewarded him with a small coin. The next day along came another child with another stone avocado, and he told me the same story. He had found it in the earth where the bulldozer was working. The next day more people brought different stone fruits – lychee and guava. I was so puzzled I took a hacksaw and cut an avocado in half. It was stone all right, but it was also fruit. I could see the lines of the fibres, and an imprint in stone of a worm that had burrowed into the fruit.' The father had none of the fruit left, having given it away over the years to people who promised to test its age, but who never contacted him again.

The day grew hot, I could hear the hiss of a slow puncture but it had not yet reached the point when the problem of a leak became more serious than the difficulty of finding the hole. I allowed the current to spin me in an enchanted circle and watched fountains of arching bamboo thirty metres tall.

For a while I paddled in company with a brace of canoes laden with fibrous planks of palm trunk which are used as slats for house walls. The canoes were lashed together and directed by an old man steering from the back. Others plied to and fro as ferries across the river near villages.

In the old days the *katibo* were said to be able to walk across the water, and I heard various tales about groups waiting for a ferry while a *katibo* in a hurry went secretly into the bushes and then materialised on the far bank, while others were said to walk openly across. In the sacred book it also said they could fly and could throw lightning. My informant told me someone had recently been arrested for throwing lightning. It sounded a violent skill but I like learning magic recipes and was pleased to add this one to my collection. It involved mixing some wood-dust from a tree that had been split by lightning, with two stones broken by lightning, soil struck by it, and powder from rotten wood from a tree whose top has been struck. To this add powder of the Lanimahery bush (whose name means Annihilated by the Powerful One), and some mud from where a quagmire quakes underfoot, so victims will tremble fearfully, and mix it with the drops of condensation under a cooking-pot's lid, which are called 'Tears that cause storm-clouds to gather'. The droplets and sooty lid represent the stormy sky, brewing the lightning. The final essentials are the tail of the water snake 'Master of the water' (Tompondrano) and the tail of the land snake 'Master of the Earth' (Tompontany). The ritual of making this magic compound is complicated but no one ever said it was easy to throw lightning.

Feeling light-hearted I took a swim alongside the canoe then lay back and floated downriver, watching the alto-stratus popples of cloud with fluffy cumulus below. The sky was above and below me, its reflection rippling with the movement of the canoe as I struggled to climb back aboard in midriver.

A couple of bottleneck squeezes with big eddies were the best the river provided in terms of action. One was a squeeze between cliffs where my canoe was pushed sideways and suddenly the surface was all eddies and small whirlpools.

The Antaimoro and other tribes kept to their separate villages, sometimes even existing side by side but preserving their separate identities. One that I passed in my canoe was the village of Ankaribary which had once taken in refugees from the land of a king who had a reputation for wisdom and being able to answer whatever question his subjects posed him. Perhaps he grew fed up with people asking stupid questions to test his ability, but when a woman was brought to him on the brink of childbirth to ask whether the child would be a boy or girl, he ordered her abdomen to be slit open, then he inspected the baby and declared its sex. His subjects were appalled by his actions and the ensuing unrest ending in the king's death, meant many fled the region.

At Ankaribary they were welcomed and given houses and a feast of welcome, after which the friendly villagers suggested a dance. But the newcomers refused to dance because their king was dead, and so they became known on the riverbank as *'tsy man dihy'* or 'those who do not dance'.

The most mysterious village I heard about was Andrebebe. Children from the village went to a nearby school and for years the teachers kept trying to find the village but with no success. The early missionaries had done no better. All reported the same thing. 'You follow the children going home and after some time there's a fog and you cannot see them any more.' Pilots have overflown the area and from the plane you can see the village exactly where it is supposed to be, with smoke coming up from the huts. They can also see the wreck of a plane from a missionary expedition that crashed looking for the village.

I was surprised to pass beneath patches of virgin forest. It seemed odd they had not been chopped down like their surroundings. But I discovered this was because they contained burial areas and were protected by *fady*. No one was allowed to chop down trees there, not even to collect windfall firewood, nor gather the fruit, nor hunt there, making each patch a haven for small-range wildlife and birds.

Corpses were brought here by canoe, and instead of being buried, were put in a special canoe which was hung from the tree branches with a pottery urn underneath to catch the drips as the body decomposed. The pots were later buried separately from the bones in the patches of forest. Each grave was marked by a stone with bits of wood covering the pot from sight.

The river became broader and shallower, moving towards the ocean. As I approached some islands a man called out 'I like your ship'. He cautioned me about crocodiles and said last month a little girl was caught here, and before that a fisherman's leg was bitten off. It didn't stop the population from bathing in the river, though.

Never had I seen so many naked men! As I floated quietly downriver in the late afternoon it was the daily bath time and naked men stood by every rock, busy with their soap and splashings. At last I arrived back in Vohipeno and, since the canoe park was near my *hotely*, I took mine there to dry off, and that evening went to meet Paulin's family and see his poultry. His pay as guide was just enough to buy a female turkey. Afterwards I had supper at the mission with Père Vincent, and went back to my *hotely* to deflate and roll up my canoe. I was at the end of my stay in Vohipeno and found a lift back to Tana.

FOUR

The Tsingy

11

At last I was heading west for the Tsingy de Bemaraha, the strange limestone pinnacle region which showed up some years ago on satellite photos. It is a World Heritage Site, which means it has been classified by the UN in the same category as sites of historical importance or architecture like the largest man-made monument on earth, Borobadur in Indonesia, which I visited in 1980. The *tsingy* has attracted recent scientific forays and the terrain is said to be so wild and difficult you cannot get across it. It sounded like my kind of place. I'm always happier not to arrive too quickly.

I had also read the legend of a tribe of white pygmies called Vazimba who had been Madagascar's first inhabitants, and had retreated into remote places when other migrant tribes arrived. The idea of white pygmies struck me as more than absurd. My normally logical friends in Tana, Moïse and Dany, told me that Vazimba do still exist but are invisible! Their homes are in caves under the *tsingy*, they communicate by telepathy and can read your thoughts. If you are on the same wavelength as them you may see them. Parents teach their children to be afraid of the Vazimba; if you do wrong, the Vazimba will make something bad happen to you. Moïse is a modern warrior with a romantic imagination.

There were no other passengers at seven a.m. in the airport waiting room, though a couple turned up at the last minute. The plane was a weekly Twin Otter which provides scheduled services to grass airstrips. The whole of western Madagascar is emptier than the highlands. Lying on the lee side of the highlands, it has seven to eight months without rain.

Below us was a desolate hell of dry burnt laterite, leached of any nutrients. In parts it supported patches of coarse dry grass. It was cattle market day at Tsiroanomandidy where we landed to pick up passengers. Their monthly cattle market is the largest in Madagascar, much of it said to be supplied by rustlers in the west's lawless zones. Without roads or communications, the area I was going to was cut off to the south because the river ferries were broken. It could be reached by walking for two days from Antsalova or by river pirogue from Ankavandra. I opted for the latter.

I knew that the Tsingy de Bemaraha was closed to outsiders, but scientists could get approval for a special permit. Not being a scientist I couldn't make a proper application but was given a letter authorising me to visit villages on both sides of the *tsingy*.

At Ankavandra we made a bumpy grass landing. The airstrip had no road to it, not even an ox-cart waiting for us, just a few young people who said they were baggage transporters. There was a five-kilometre bush footpath to the town, and a large river to cross. This was the river I planned to canoe down. To cross it, we had to wade. I tucked my skirt to the top of my legs but was soon waist-deep. The porters balanced my luggage on their heads. I was soaked. The local people simply carried their *lambas* across and retied them on the far bank.

Ankavandra was a no-horse town but it boasted a school and a Catholic mission. I was invited to stay with the headmistress Eleanore and her husband Toro and, to my astonishment, they both spoke fluent English. Normally it's difficult even to find someone who can speak French. A delightful couple, they were from the plateau and had come here some years ago to start a new life. Eleanore had previously been teaching English at the lycée in Tana, but city life was tough and Toro wanted their children to grow up in the countryside, so they searched for a member of either family to give them the territorial right to live in another tribal region. Finally they located an uncle in Ankavandra. Apart from her school work, Eleanore also runs a café/restaurant, and they let me rent a room at their house.

Toro offered his services as a river guide, together with a friend and his pirogue, warning me of rocky gorges that demanded local expertise. An extra paddler would have to be hired to share the work. I had already come to the conclusion that my small canoe would be overladen, so we negotiated a price and agreed to leave the day after next. Toro guessed the trip would take three or four days, and my map showed it as further than I'd thought.

Fresh supplies needed to be added to my dried food rations, but the market was stupendously empty, no fruit or veg, only some rice being sold by young women. Eleanore said that, apart from a few Christians, most women in Ankavandra don't bother to marry. The rest simply cohabit and change partner when they feel like it. Girls from fifteen years old try to get pregnant to prove their fertility and score a better mate.

This is not the land of milk and honey, it swelters in 30–40°c heat for most of the year. 'And for three months it's so hot we can't move. We've no energy for anything except to lie in the shade. That's what happens, the whole place falls asleep for months on end. Except after dark when the moon rises. Like most of Madagascar we don't have electricity so the moonlight is important to us. It's our light, a natural light. When there is moonlight we call each other to dance. Children play and people sing.' And Eleanore sang me a moonlight song: 'The moon is shining and calls us to play, to play; the stars and the clouds are waving to us. The sound of the wind is whispering everywhere, it calls us to play. We call each other, come, come, come to play. All of you, yes you who have troubles, let's enjoy ourselves; you, yes you who are sorrowful, let's play quickly.'

The Catholic missionary, Père Jeremy, joined us for supper and Eleanore spread a tasty feast of chicken, egg and tomato. Père Jeremy is Canadian and had worked some years in Antsalova beside the *tsingy*, and when I asked if he had seen Vazimba he told me 'They see you but you don't see them.' Not you, too, I thought. But he went on, between solemnly munching his chicken. 'Sometimes they come to market, but you won't know who they are. They're supposed to be the original people of Madagascar. Not indigenous, of course, they must have come from somewhere. And they carry on existing in pockets so remote you would never know they were there. They're very shy, and no one has ever caught one.'

Equally secretive but much more violent are the cattle rustlers who roam the region. Its remoteness and vast empty savannah make the enforcement of law and order a non-starter. Some rustling has become big business, or organised crime, run from the capital. It began with the idea of destabilising the previous government and proved to be so lucrative it has flourished. Many stolen cattle are herded to the coast across much of the area I was planning to visit, and shipped alive to Mauritius and Réunion. Others, as I had seen, are walked to Tsiroanomandidy for sale at the market. Normally no one sells cattle, they are kept for emergencies and rituals. So at least banditry ensures a supply of meat to the markets in Tana.

Toro said the groups are armed with Kalashnikovs and are willing to use them, but one time they had helped him across bad terrain and shared their food with him. I couldn't believe they would have any reason to bother a foreigner. The pirogue crew turned up but without the pirogue, saying the river was too rough and no one had been down it since the last cyclone. This was a gambit to score more pay, which we resolved. As for the river, Toro assured me there was no great danger if we were careful.

Supplies were supplemented with a bottle of rum – for the river. A drop would be poured into the water at our departure and a bit more when we reached certain testing points. I sat in the early sun at the river's edge, waiting for a lad to bring the pirogue and watching a woman in yellow rags rinsing and wringing bright orange *lambas*. Various people waded across the river, one with a song.

The pirogue arrived half-full of water, so while the lad bailed it out, I helped Toro find short logs to keep the baggage off the wet floor. The rum ceremony involved a long speech to the sacred river Manambolo which ended with a request to be kept safe through the sacred gorge. Then we all made the motions of rubbing water on our heads and drinking some rum. I noticed it was not poured in the water. A teetotal sacred river? Perhaps this was why we got stuck on a sandbank within the first kilometre. After two hours we had covered only three kilometres on my map. We had planned to do sixty in the day. But I wasn't worried, it didn't matter to me how many days the voyage lasted.

The current was not fast and, being quite shallow, some bits made a lot of noise without danger. I was amused to see we usually headed for the roughest bits. Its course meandered widely leaving ox-bow lakes and shallow mudbanks, backed by crumpled hills of empty and burnt red laterite. We came to a wild west landscape of eroded plugs, purple-topped, brick red at their waists

The amazing limestone world of the Tsingy de Bemaraha.

The *tsingy* is classed as a World Heritage Site. An aerial view is breathtaking, closer to progress is perilous.

Above, my zebu chariot, a means of transport in Sakalava regions; below left, local musicians celebrating Independence Day. The *jejy voatavo* (right) has a gourd resonator and two sets of strings on the neck; below right, a Beosy tribesman, said to be the remnants of an earlier race which settled on the island before the Malagasy arrived.

A night market in Antsalova town square, western Madagascar.

Some of Madagascar's remarkable range of wildlife: sifaka lemurs, one of the most graceful of the island's thirty-eight species; crocodile custodians of ancestor spirits; chameleons keep one eye on the past and one on the future and catch their prey with the reflex action of their long sticky tongues; the ploughshare tortoise, one of the world's rarest, with a baby radiator tortoise; the leaf-tailed gecko.

A Merina turning of the bones celebration when the bodies of the ancestors are brought out of the tomb for a joyful family reunion and rewrapping.

A Merina ancestor receives a new shroud with all the family lending a hand.

Above, race day at last. The author, in red with a blue helmet, came fifth; below, Jonah sitting in one of the world's largest petrified forests, another of Madagascar's well kept secrets.

fading to white bases, with not a cloud in the sky, except for the odd wispy puff above a plug.

Occasionally in the bareness along the riverside there were leafy patches of tamarind and mango. Other river traffic was nonexistent. Birdlife consisted of one heron and a falcon. The river squeezed between pale bluffs, and we floated over the turbulence. The old piroguier at the front was never sure which channel to follow but Toro's advice was confident, and the lad at the back provided sturdy muscles. For him it was a first descent. He had been a ferry-boy until now, and was a promisingly good lad who would benefit from this experience. He said that during the last cyclone he was almost swamped when he was canoeing across the river and was afraid he would die.

Two gold panners had been drowned already this year. They were not local and didn't know the river. They were swept away and the bodies found far downstream. The rewards for gold hunters are hard earned, carrying earth and rocks to wash for nuggets at the riverbank in summer and panning alluvial gold all winter. The local Sakalava people don't bother with such work, they are pastoralists and only interested in their herds of cattle. Toro said few Sakalava have been to school, they don't like contact with the outside world, fearing its invasion and the diseases it brings. They want their children to look after cattle, and be able to tell the health of a cow by feeling its skin. They said they have nothing to learn from education.

This was the time of year for setting bushfires to clear the coarse old grass and generate fresh new growth for the cattle in spring. They said it was their duty. I could see fires burning on two hillsides. The tragedy of this custom is that when the grass is burnt there is nothing to stop the wash-off of soil in the heavy rains.

The day was hot and I was grateful for a breeze and for occasional patches of shade where trees hung out over the water. Their branches were laden with driftwood and dead grass clumps caught there when the river was in flood. The January high watermark was four metres above us.

Beside Madagascar's rivers there are legends about disappearing children who return after some days saying they have been with the water-people. By the next day they remember nothing of it. Sometimes the child brought back meat or flowers, or gold jewellery, given them by these water-people who provided whatever the children asked for, and when the children asked to go home, they allowed that too. The children said life was better with the water-people but they missed their families too much.

Water-babies was the name for still-born infants who, by custom, were buried in marshes inside big clay pots, as if still in the mother's womb. The pot used would be the mother's main kitchen water-pot. The infants could not be buried in dry earth because they had not lived to become dry – they were water-babies.

We were now running along the base of a long range of hills and endlessly changing sides of the river to find the best channel. Eddies went upstream as fast as the current went down. We went briefly ashore to collect more sticks to hold the baggage above the wet floor and as we reboarded Toro offered the proverbs 'Once you have both feet in the canoe, you cannot step back' and 'Do not kick away the canoe which helped you to cross the river'.

A group of lemurs was asleep in a tree, and further on a crocodile dozed on a sandbank, which provoked the old man to contribute his proverb: 'When many people cross the river together, croco-diles do not eat them.' The instant this one heard the canoe it dived off the bank into the river. Only a small one, the old man said. He'd seen them bigger than our canoe, at five metres, but few are left nowadays.

The crocodile is considered sacred in much of Madagascar, like the snake, for the ancestral spirits it possesses. When a crocodile comes peacefully into a riverside village, it will be offered things to eat, usually a hen with tied legs. A speech is made to the crocodile, 'Dear grandparent, we are happy that you visit us, please accept this gift. Please give us your blessing and go quietly back to your home in the river.' As elsewhere, people are afraid of them and they are known to kill the odd zebu.

When crossing a dangerous part of the river in a ferry canoe, he warned me the custom was that you should not speak, keeping your mouth closed and teeth clenched. Open mouths suggest the open jaws of crocodiles. And you never wear red clothes to cross the river, because it is seen as a challenge, as is to touch the water with iron.

Toro pointed out an illegal crocodile trap by a creek, a noose mechanism baited with scrag of zebu. Apart from the considerable value of the skin, the fat under the skin is sold as a medicine against asthma. The crocodiles semi-hibernate in the dry season, burying themselves in the reeds and mud by the river, and while they sleep the reeds grow over them. When the crocodile eventually moves from this bed, the mat of reeds stays glued to his back and for some days he looks like a moving island.

In the local myths department Toro told me about a creature looking like a long-haired girl with long fingernails who steals meat from the camp-kitchen at night when you are sleeping. Few people can describe her because she is quick to run away, but enough have seen her to insist that she is real. In Toro's opinion she is a lemur, one of the upright sifaka types. This place is a paradise for lemurs; half of all types of lemurs that live in Madagascar are found in this area.

So what, I asked, about the Vazimba? Toro offered the idea that they come to this river in winter when the water is low, like now. He said he knew of a Vazimba cave tomb in the side of the gorge which he would show me at the end of our voyage.

We camped that first night on an idyllic sandbank by the river and sunset faded into a very starry night. I killed my first scorpion, a sandy-brown one which was probably attracted towards the candlelight as I wrote my diary.

The days developed their own pattern, up at dawn, the men cooked rice, broke camp and loaded the canoe, then we made unhurried progress downriver. Toro was always good company, and the lad frequently sang songs, sometimes drumming an accompaniment on the side of the canoe, or power-paddling us forward with great surging thrusts. I felt sunburnt, happy, dirty and my backpack gear was full of sand.

At a particularly shallow section we could see where cattle had recently crossed the river but Toro said it was not the big time cattle rustlers – the *dahalo*. These were just local poachers who they have to endure as a fact of life. Everyone knows who they are, these cocks of the village or 'petits machos'. But the *dahalo* are mafiosi, running a calculated and well organised racket.

On the third day there was a noticeable slope to the riverbed as it began the descent to the big gorge. A submerged sandbar made our course hazardous and my crew fell silent while all three plied their paddles.

Apart from flowing downhill, the current also snaked from side to side and corkscrewed top to bottom, leaving its surface one moment glassy smooth then a mass of spinning bubbling eddies. The lad sang and paddled with extra gusto. Ahead of us the river squeezed through a bottleneck with waves we could hear but not see. Soon we could see the waves churning over an obstacle. All paddles going, the men called urgent instructions to each other as we went into a maelstrom of currents. My consternation was only to notice we were heading for the worst patch, as usual. With three strong men nothing is really a problem and we slid safely through to ride on the V-waves.

The walls of the canyon slowly came closer together, a two-tiered canyon, I kept waiting to enter the sacred gorge but despite passing through several natural gates as the river cut through hills, the canyon stayed wide. Toro said this region was below sealevel many millions of years ago, which is how the *tsingy* was formed. He himself had never been to the *tsingy*. He pointed to some mounded tombs by the river and told me they were reputed to be Vazimba, and added that the Vazimba burial caves we would see later in the river gorge were only accessible from the water.

'You see that big cave high up in the cliff? It is said that one day a man took his son-in-law there to collect vampire bats for food. From the cliff top the man ordered his daughter's husband to climb down to the cave on a rope. The youth reached the cave and gathered the vampires in a bag, and attached it to the rope. His father-in-law pulled up the rope, took the bag of bats, and didn't lower the rope again. He left the youngster there to die.'

Quickly Toro gestured to a shadow where a man was hiding beside a tree. We all saw him, hiding and obviously afraid. 'Maybe he thinks we're gendarmes,' said Toro and called him a *kazak* which means a man like a wild animal.

Finally we were in the gorge, the great cliffs towered to both sides and their depths hung with stalactites, some with mosses and

ferns trailing down from them. The air was cool. My lads were
totally silent, they refused to speak because of the sacredness of the
place. It merited its status; everything was larger and greater than
us. We were down at the very bottom, the lowest level, above us
the dripping stalactites, the cliffs, forest and taller cliffs above.

When we reached the Vazimba caves we clambered ashore
and up a steep landslide against the cliff which had exposed
the interior of one of the caves. At a shallow overhang we had
another rum ceremony. I counted ten skulls there, and there
were also piles of small hollowed out canoe-like logs containing more bones and skull fragments, all gleaming whitely. Toro
told me these were coffins, but they were far too small, unless for children or for bones to be collected after the body
had rotted away. He agreed no adult would fit the coffins and
when I tried a leg bone against him for size, it was much his
height. So if these were Vazimba bones they did not belong
to a pygmy race. I was struck by the oddness of being surrounded by all these vertebrae, ribs and thigh bones – bits of a
mythical people who had lived and died in a time that has been
forgotten.

As we floated away from the caves we came into sight of
Bekopaka's landing beach with its rusting defunct pontoon ferry.
So, leaving the canoe and two-man crew at the beach, Toro and
I walked the three kilometres in to town which was just as small
as Ankavandra, but sleepier and dustier. Toro bought supplies
for the pirogue's return journey and then said goodbye. He had
been a most unexpected and delightful companion. I found the
hotel, which had five rooms and was run by an entrepreneur
called Ibrahim, and I joined him and his wife for a supper
of delicious wild duck, since there were no other guests. The
kitchen boy had been taught to cook by Ibrahim's wife, and she
knew some unusually tasty dishes.

Afterwards I cleaned the sand from my gear and made contact
with a diffident young man called Haja who worked for the UN
Development Fund in the *tsingy*. He took me to a patch of *tsingy*
bordering the river, a smaller scale version of what lay ahead.
In parts where the ground should have been there was a mass
of deep pockets and bridges, with blocks of *tsingy* sticking up

from deep underground, the spear-headed points soaring into the air.

In order to survive in this extraordinary no-ground environment the plants have adapted elongated tentacle stems, pushing their leaves towards the sunlight, while those that grow on peaks send down their roots in search of moisture, sometimes plunging thirty metres before finding damp humus. The soil is purely vegetable, made of leaves and rotted wood. In the deepest pockets are plants that can not tolerate sunshine.

I was in a crack in the rock just wider than my shoulders, the rock worn smooth by floodwaters but still with plenty of hand- and foot-holds. Thick roots dangled past me, but they were not good holds since they were too elastic and kept stretching.

This place was called the Canyon des Beriha which means many levels. It had probably been home to the Vazimba whose burial cave I'd visited. Haja said that Vazimba started the tradition of cattle theft and the area has always had a bad reputation. Local Sakalava used it as a cattle thieves' hideout 300 to 400 years ago.

We were underground beneath two great rocks that had fallen sideways, fifteen metres tall, forming a triangle of cave with light spilling in. This cave was reserved for *trumba* trances, when the spirits of the past were invoked in those present, an important aspect of the Sakalava cult of the dead. From the cave of trances we clambered down out through a gap in the bottom, using my torch, a four-storey descent, rocks rattling away from our feet into an abyss ahead. I could hear them plopping into water below.

This permanent well meant a subterranean village could exist and we found broken pottery in all the caves; several families had lived there. I found a lovely piece of an urn with parallel line design, and a finer thinner piece with zigzags at the top. Haja explained that the inhabitants lived here before alphabeticism reached Madagascar. 'We never find script here, only geometric motifs. Some pots were used to cook in, and there look, are cavities in the rock that were used as kitchens.' He pointed out the soot-blackened ceilings and hearths. We chimneyed down a rock shaft, feet against one side, bum against the other, down to a deep dark lake. The water was utterly still, with a pinnacle in the middle. It was possible to traverse along the vertical side above the water, as there were plenty of handholds, but the rock was so sharp it scraped the skin. Then we wriggled on stomach and peeled elbows under a smooth overhang, worn by an old river, and came out into the sunshine again.

The Canyon des Beriha was outside the Reserve limits, and the main area of *tsingy* where I was heading lay a day's walk to the north of the town of Bekopaka. But things began to go wrong for me at the UNESCO project office in town. My authorisation letter was not enough. Without clearance I would not see the Great Tsingy. There was nothing for it but to go the whole bureaucratic route and obtain the permit, but this would take a week or two.

In this great plain without roads there seemed to be just one vehicle, Ibrahim's jeep, which had just been commandeered by the military. They had been chasing *dahalo* and were returning in triumphant mood to Belo. I hitched a lift for the night-long ride while they regaled me with their heroics. The week before they had caught a group of twenty bandits and others were killed in the shoot-out. There were no losses among the soldiers, but the bandit chief had escaped. The captured men would be sent for trial at Maintirano. As for the cattle, it sounded to me like they were being kept by the gendarmes.

The bandits built temporary camps in the Bemaraha forests and moved frequently to avoid detection. They carried modern weapons and were bold enough to attack villages in broad daylight. Usually they let the villagers know beforehand so they could flee, leaving their cattle to be stolen on pain of the village being destroyed. Any person who attempted to retrieve stolen zebu brought further attacks on his village.

For the villagers, there was no security whatsoever, and it was not unknown for the brigands to abduct local women out searching for water or roots. For the law enforcers it was hard to know who was a bandit and who wasn't, since anyone with a grudge against someone else might report him as being *dahalo*. In Bekopaka people told me they felt safe but only because of the protection of a big bandit whose family lived in the town.

A tangle of rifles bounced around with us in the back of the jeep. They were in working order but not modern. In the old

days, guns and muskets were kept more for ceremonial purposes, carried as decoration more than to intimidate. Their use
as weapons was so unreliable that spears were often preferred for
the serious business of killing someone.

The drive was magnificent for its awfulness. It tunnelled through
the forest, and across grasslands, the road indistinguishable in the
tall dry grass. We got stuck in a muddy stream for an hour, despite
twelve pairs of heaving muscles. I saw a surprising number of
snakes, mostly boa constrictors.

At midnight we arrived by chance at the wake of a man who
died the day before. His body was laid out in the house and
his family were gathering. Four girls danced in the firelight,
not elegantly with hands and feet, they just stood jiggling their
whole body. One girl had orange beauty-spots painted on her
face, and another had the typical Sakalava hairstyle of many
large buns like knobs on her head.

The Muslim call to prayer coincided with the crowing of the
town cocks as I fell asleep at dawn in Belo. It was still too soon
to expect my permit for the *tsingy*, so I was going to look at some
tombs on the coast. It took one and a half hours by pirogue from
Belo to cross the Tsiribina delta, from where I could drop to the
sea. Tombs are scattered all along this coast and to the south.

This obsession with death and tombs is not mine, it is Malagasy
and a reflection of the way the ancestors permeate daily life. That
said, I must admit I was becoming fascinated by the diversity of
Malagasy burial rites I had learnt about so far, and I looked
forward to the turning of the bones ceremony I had been invited
to attend in six weeks' time. Here in the west there were different
ceremonies. After crossing a dry floodplain and some lagoons
beside the ocean I visited two superb collections of Vezo graves
with wooden *aloalo* or totem poles depicting people and animals,
and further south they were carved as a single naked figure from
which rose a post of geometric shapes topped by birds symbolising
peace, or zebu with fat humps. The most elaborate posts I saw
were for Mahafaly people and had carved scenes taken from
daily life. One was of a zebu being eaten by a crocodile and
another of people in a canoe which perhaps commemorated someone who drowned when a canoe overturned.

One has to be careful not to break taboos around graves, and if one does, one has to atone by giving the injured family a chicken or some eggs; the number depends on the seriousness of the offence, or, in reality, on the availability of chickens or eggs.

Some funerary sculpture portrayed the deceased person and events in his life, or aspects of his character. A man at his desk could have been a clerk, one with cap and rifle was a soldier, and one by a football goal post was a sportsman. The sculptures like birds of peace or painted aeroplanes were to reflect the process of death. The word *aloalo* means intermediary or messenger and the purpose of the sculpture was to give honour and help elevate the dead to join the ancestors.

Some Sakalava *aloalo* went in for erotic poses, judoesque embraces with exaggerated sexual parts. These were not done as a likeness, the Malagasy are modest. So they were either intended to promote the fertility of the surviving family, or were a notice of rebirth into the world of ancestors.

South of Belo and still with time to kill I revisited one of my favourite haunts, the majestic bulbous baobab tree area; the mere sight of such trees lifts my spirits. I'd been told that many baobabs had been knocked over by a cyclone a few years ago, but I found they were regenerating, not dead, and from the roots of the fallen trees new shoots had pushed up. It is said in legends that baobab trees live for ever, and I remembered once counting the rings on a section of trunk, and working out it was up to 850 years old. People do not cut into or harm the baobab, but they often cut off swathes of bark for house building. There are even some dwellings inside baobab trees. One-room homes have been dug and hollowed out inside their bloated trunks, without killing the tree. The kitchen area would be just outside the trunk.

I stayed in a village among the baobabs with a lady who kept chickens and watched how she fed them. It was beautifully simple. She went to one of the nearby termite hills and, lifting off its earthen cap, took out a cloth crawling with termites. This she gave to the chickens who wasted no time in polishing off the termites. She meanwhile had poked another cloth into their hill, smeared with something like honey to attract more termites. The chickens' cupboard would never be empty.

One of the baobabs had notches up its trunk, to do with fixing nets to catch fruit bats which are eaten by the villagers.

There are six different species of baobab in Madagascar, while Africa has but one. A young scientist friend from Switzerland, Urs Thalman, said he thought there was a new species of baobab on the plateau de Bemaraha. He was waiting for the leaves and flowers to show to be certain. They could be different because baobabs usually like sandy ground, not calcareous rock. Madagascar's wealth of new species is extraordinary in today's world. Urs's project, like Deborah's in Ranomafana, was lemur research and on his first visit, like Deborah's, he had helped find a new species. Instead of the hairless black faced mask of a sifaka, the cat-sized nocturnal one he saw had a hairy face, also an unusually long tail and different limb proportions.

The lemur researchers I met were not all foreigners. The remarkable Malagasy, Gilbert Rahelivololona was studying the aye-aye, which I consider the ugliest of the lemurs, with a face like an alien from Mars, coarse black hair, bat ears and a fox's tail, a lemur designed by a committee. Its skeletal index finger which is used to hook grubs out of holes in trees is prized as a fetish by sorcerers. Having been considered almost extinct because it had not been seen in the wild for five years, it was found in healthy numbers in the 1980s by the naturalist Liz Bomford who said it was always there but the scientists looked for it in the wrong places and at the wrong times. Now thought to exist in many habitats, Gilbert's job was to establish its distribution.

I enjoy listening to such people because their work is pioneer stuff, breaking new ground. Gilbert described night after night of crawling around looking for aye-aye, losing heart with the fruitlessness of searching in the dry forests of the south-west. But when he reported failure to his bosses, they just told him to go back and try again.

He combed the forest further south with no success until one night. 'The night I found the aye-aye, I danced among the trees laughing with happiness.'

12

By mid-June I had been granted a permit for the *tsingy*, with freedom to go anywhere in the 152,000 hectare Reserve area. The place which had seemed for me to be one that moved further off as I approached, was now only twenty-four hours away. The permit was valid for a month, so I chose two directions, firstly the *tsingy* stretching north of Bekopaka, including the Great Tsingy, and later I would go up near Antsalova to the Beboka River *tsingy*. Although the Project was not keen on tourism it wanted to promote scientific interest and I was allowed in because the radio series I was making about Madagascar for the BBC was mainly about national heritage and natural phenomena; my permit read 'for purpose of recording sounds'.

As before, I based myself in Bekopaka at Ibrahim's small hotel, then went round to the Project office and presented my permit to my friend Haja, who arranged for a guide called Tsihalala, Tsi for short, to accompany me for the next week.

A track led to Ambalarano village but there was no road to the *tsingy*, its isolation being its best defence, that and the lack of water. The villagers had hidden the whereabouts of their water source from all outsiders until the first organised survey of the *tsingy* in 1990.

We walked along a contour parallel to the distant line of cliffs and down across grasslands dotted with wild lupin-plants in yellow flower. Two small snakes moved out of the way but I stopped when I saw one as fat as my arm coming out of a hole in the ground just ahead of me. Tsi said it could bite but was not dangerous because Malagasy snakes have no poison. I stamped my foot and the serpent coiled back and returned to its hole. Later we saw a boa, almost three metres long and fawn coloured with black markings on its back. There are a lot of them here, they are tolerated around villages because they keep down the rats. Boa constrictors are only found in Madagascar and South America, which defies one to work out how.

At the base of the cliff, the Falaise de Bemaraha, the going was tougher with dry swamp forest where we moved bent double, and thorn bush which tore at our clothes and skin with curved hooks. Even the creepers had hairy pods that stung if you brushed against them. The cliff wall was a sharp jagged mass of rock needles and razor edges, here reaching fifteen metres tall and going back into the no-ground chaos I remembered from my previous short excursion with Haja. After walking twenty-four kilometres I was pleased to make camp where the *tsingy* cliff meets the plain of Ambalarano. Tsi knew where to find water in a source beneath the rocks, and lowered a bucket on a string. He was born and raised in this area and when I asked him about the Vazimba he said he was half-Vazimba himself and both his grandfathers were pure Vazimba.

'As a child I used to come here with my father and grandpa to look for honey and go hunting, and to the east we raised zebu. Honey is easy to find. Even today you only have to follow the bees, and let them lead you to their hive. To take the honey we light a small fire by the entrance so the bees will move off. But we make sure not to disturb the bit with the eggs, the larva and any young hatching bees and after I've taken what I want, I close the hole a little to reassure the bees, so they will stay there. Honey gathering has always been a Vazimba custom.'

He went on to describe other wild foods found deep in the *tsingy*, including a tuber-like sweet potato a metre long, and various wild fruits.

Tsi's grandfather was born just beside the *tsingy*, following a seasonal pattern of moving between rocks and plain according to water availability. All Vazimba retreated inside the *tsingy* when strangers were seen, especially during the whole French colonisation period. They wanted nothing to do with that. Those who didn't live in caves under the *tsingy* built temporary shelters of branches and leaves, collapsible without trace of their existence. Their blankets and clothes were made from the bark of the Devula tree. Most of this region's inhabitants have Vazimba blood. He added that Ibrahim's wife where I had stayed in Bekopaka is a full-blood Vazimba.

The new moon lit the clifftop, and our camp was shared by an owl. I was woken at dawn by the 'oua oua si-faka' cry of a sifaka lemur bounding into the tree above me and peering down, the black muzzle slanting inquisitively.

To get inside the *tsingy* we climbed up a worn dry streambed to a short canyon and traversed the side of a nasty deep fissure, treading from one needle of rock to the next. The next few hours had the adrenalin pumping with the knowledge that any wrong footing could be disastrous, combined with the pure enchantment of being in another world.

From inside one impressive fissure I could see narrow tunnels going off and an open-topped cavern with pandanus palms growing at the base. I rested for a moment on the edge of a sheer vertical chasm and, lobbing a stone into the crack, I heard it bounce from wall to wall eternally down. This disturbed a flock of bats that swarmed up around us squeaking, so we edged along a shelf which opened out into a theatre of pillars and pinnacles.

A network of underground rivers, seasonal and now dry, crisscrossed the massif and we sometimes used their courses to walk along. Coming up from one we hugged the vertical side of a ravine and had to cross to the other side, crawling on a precarious bridge of rock above a mind-boggling drop into deep black needles. Then we edged up a wall that had slivers of rock peeling away from it. The slivers were strong enough to cling to but razor sharp. Our feet had to seek the spear points reaching sideways and up with our toes. The noise when you tap the rock is a brittle clinking, almost resonant, and Tsi said the word *tsingy* describes that sound. Remembering some rudimentary rock climbing lessons, I kept counting to three, checking that I had three points of contact with the rockface, and not moving hand or foot until I'd checked my holds.

My intention today was to reach the Roof of the *Tsingy*, where the needles flatten out enough for walking. It took a couple of hours and I had one fall, a non-serious but timely warning. But it was worth the struggle and is justly designated a site of World Heritage. The roof overlooks a sea of pinnacles, some like cathedrals, with thirty-metre spires. It is an awesome sight.

A flat section along the plateau edge allowed us to roam north and south, jumping various cracks that dropped either to blackness or to pockets or stilt-legged vegetation.

On the roof grew types of plants I had not seen before. Few plants can adapt to such dryness and here were some of the ten types of pachypodium, which store water in their squat trunks to last through the long dry season. They look withered and thin by the end. The smallest pachypodium is the size of a tennis ball with stems from it like arms ending in springtime in yellow flowers. The leaves are pinky-violet and now dropping off so the plant would not lose water by transpiration. Another almost as small, like a pincushion, has knobs and spines. It needs spines since it has a spongy coat and no bark fibre. The only endemic cactus of Madagascar looks more like mistletoe than cactus. The Rapsillus is an epiphyte not a parasite and it never has leaves, being a mass of green stems that do the job of leaves. Most colourful on the teeth of the roof were Kalanchoes with orange bell-flowers, elegant on tall necks. At the tips of the fleshy base leaves were mini-plantlets complete with tiny roots that would drop off and grow nearby in an asexual type of reproduction.

Half a kilometre to the south I found a cirque of horizontally banded rock in uneven layers, worn through underneath to form a monumental archway with two tunnels to the light beyond.

The interest to both science and heritage is because this rockscape exists nowhere but Madagascar, except for a patch of it in China which I visited in 1984. But that was small and well-worn by comparison with here. How such shapes were formed was not clear, though obviously sedimentary. It seemed to me that the long Bemaraha cliff line must have once been part of the coast aeons ago and was eroded by wave action; in lower tunnels I often found seashells underfoot. Another curiosity were the seemingly fossilised imprints of anemone-like starfish and flowery sponges.

The days blurred together, we moved camp a couple of times and made various journeys inside the *tsingy*. Just south of us was a wide canyon, both walls honeycombed with multi-level caves leading towards other parts. High-level aerial photos showed the canyon running east–west, so from the western exit we followed it back, cutting deep through the *tsingy*. The canyon floor was dry forest, pandanus and tall thin trunks heading for the sky. We hit debris of major rockfalls and chutes leading into the pothole system below. In the first big cave we went down a slide of batshit and down a rockfall to where a choice of passages led off into darkness. These were tall passages, wide enough to walk in, and sometimes you would see light coming from far above, and sometimes you disturbed bats.

My second cave yielded greater depths, five storeys down, with chinks of light illuminating galleries and stalagmites. The largest cave was a yawning mouth with a stumpy row of stalactites hanging across the entrance, blunted by the annual floods that pour into the cave and down its throat. As I prepared to go down it I noticed the tonsils, a great bulbous calcium form, encrusted with floret-shapes, glistening.

The lower chambers were vastly tall, far beyond the beam of my torch, though occasionally the beam caught curtains of stalactites. In a higher gallery I could see crusty stalactites dropping thirty metres down a root system while free-standing roots had been encased in calcium to form pillars.

Later we reached a particularly pretty area of short tunnels joining sunny glades. There were various ways on to the roof twenty metres above us, but I couldn't get an overall view, so we went into a wide north–south canyon and Tsi showed me a pool of eels. 'I used to fish at night here, the eels can be a metre long. They come out to eat the frogs.' There are over one hundred and fifty species of frog on the island, and all but two are native, but there are no toads or newts.

One thing led to another, the tunnel had a short chimney into an open-air passage, then we squeezed through a rockslide which was how we found a way onwards up the canyon, long past where Tsi or the survey had ever been. With the *tsingy* rearing up all around, it was impressive. Tsi said that only the wild honey hunters come this far and he started notching trees along our route so we would be able to find the way out. The honey hunters never left marks, they did not want anyone to know where they had been. When Tsi walked through forest, he did not break twigs or branches, and he did not fight his way along. Rather he seemed to slide through it all, leaving no trace.

We continued on into uncharted land, having come so far it was worth seeing what happened next. The problem was picking the right level to go forward as we hunted for access, sometimes up along higher storeys then down again, using roots to abseil into depths. From an open bowl in the canyon we could see we were now on the plateau of Bemaraha, and had reached the east edge of the *tsingy*.

As a traveller, I feel that you leave part of yourself in such powerful places, and you carry part of its power away in your mind or spirit. Being alone, with only a guide, means you have the place to yourself, it belongs to you for that moment in time. The memory can re-evoke the power. That's something you try to keep for ever.

We trekked south to look for a place Tsi remembered, scrambling many hours up and down rocks in dry forest. The roots that are so useful on the way up are lethal on the way down because they loop round your feet and whereas one expects to be able to kick free, these held firm like tripwires. It's the long thick roots that are stretchy. I found a set of eight different ones like harp strings across a cavern.

In pockets of forest as we climbed up rock rising through the tree canopy we would find ourselves level with the lemurs and I often stopped to watch sifakas grooming. When they leapt between trees, long hair trailing, leaping in an upright position and landing on their hind feet, it was almost a ballet for its grace and beauty. One tree we climbed through had a flock of parakeets, bright yellow-green and chirping in uproar.

A wild boar had walked through our camp while we were out, it left a pile of droppings that told us it had eaten something indigestible.

One morning in the forest I walked into a hornets' nest and got a few stings, and rubbed against the plant that itches like mad, but neither really bothered me. I guessed my arms were so scratched and grazed by climbing in the rocks I couldn't distinguish any pain in particular any more.

Tsi spotted a bees' stopover nest hanging at headlevel one pace ahead of me. The bees had woven the end leaves of a branch by clustering tightly in a long oval hub, doubtless around their queen. They writhed and crawled in a seething mass. Tsi said they had abandoned their old home, perhaps disturbed by honey hunters, and were now seeking a new place. They would stop over here as a hanging mass until their scouts found a suitable new home, then they would all move there en masse.

My shoes had been an early casualty of the *tsingy*, their soles were ripped to shreds and I frequently had to bind plastic tape round them. I worked out they would last three kilometres between repairs and luckily I had plenty of tape. The Vazimba had worn shoes of cowhide laced over their feet with thongs.

Occasionally we found caves that had been inhabited; at a series of caves along the front cliff this was obvious from the quantity of black soot from cooking fires absorbed into the rock, showing a row of hearths like semi-detached homes. They were halfway up the cliff and had a superb view over the plain.

They used to farm wild lemurs as one of their sources of food. They also ate wild boar, fish and guinea fowl. We still found plenty of flocks of guinea fowl.

We had reached an area called Andamizavaky where we found some small canyons and further south an outcrop where *tsingy* stretched inland in a huge curve in front of the cliffs, and here we rested at noon, plagued by sweat bees looking for moisture. Tsi said the only water here was very deep under the outcrop. A mongoose with long red and black banded tail scuttled past to seize a piece of fallen fruit.

Nearby on the plain I noticed some square tombs of roughly piled stones which Tsi said were Vazimba but no longer used and no one knew who were their descendents. A young snake, thinner than a pencil, lay sunbathing on one tomb, and I remembered to leave it alone because snakes carry dead spirits, and anyway to hassle a snake is asking for trouble.

Tsi's father's tomb is beside the Manambolo River. Apart from the Vazimba element, the local Sakalava are mixed with innumerable other tribes and the area is also home to the fiercer Bara and Antandroy nomadic cattle herding tribes. Bara usually carry spears. Antandroy or 'People of the Thorns' come from the arid south, dark skinned and almost naked, and have settled here keeping their own customs.

On Day Five I added a local Bara cattleherd to help as guide because Tsi and I kept losing our way. With the herdsboy we explored a whole new maze of canyons, one flanked by spear points of rock indented with numerous thin caves hung with stalactites scooped smooth by the raging yearly floods. The going was particularly jagged and the herdsboy, wriggling down a chimney in thong sandals of zebu hide he had made himself, told me about a herb you can use to stop bleeding if you cut yourself very badly. The leaves are mashed to a yellow-green pulp which not only stops blood loss but helps with regeneration of new tissue. As a herdsboy the lad said he was paid in cattle. For guarding fifty head he was earning one calf a year.

Tsi was intrigued by the place we had come to, he had not known it existed. The area had also been missed by all other exploratory forays. There were still twenty cave-tombs here, some historic and some in current use, tucked in where dense forest pressed against the cliff and hid the caves. We three sat in the outer cave of a tomb while I retaped the soles of my shoes.

'When we bring a corpse here,' the lad explained, 'we feast for a day or two on zebu, longer if the person was rich, and put the body in place with a cookpot and a bottle of water.'

The tomb behind us was full, the dead placed side by side. Though no longer in use it was not forgotten; the descendants still cared for it. True Bara descendants knew their tombs. But the Vazimba descendants didn't know theirs.

Inside the *tsingy* there are a couple more Vazimba cave-tombs and since no one except the descendants has the right to go in to them, those tombs should by rights stay sealed for ever, despite the 1990 Survey revealing the presence of copper jewellery and artefacts. Tsi regretted that Vazimba seemed so secretive that they hid everything about their lives and their dead even from their own children.

In Bekopaka and later in Antsalova I managed to piece together what must have been the history of the Vazimba, a pastoral race of migrants from Indonesia via East Africa, here long before the

Merina arrival. They roamed with their herds of cattle in the highlands. Merina oral tradition states that Tana was originally a Vazimba town called Analamangao. The new waves of immigrants pushed the Vazimba to the savannah of the west. A Vazimba chief called Rangoromana stopped at Bongolava and left no further history except for his enormous cattle herds which turned wild after his death, and are the base stock of the wild cattle around the *tsingy* today. Another Vazimba leader Voavo settled near Ankavandra and his sister Ampelamana, who had to leave because her son tried to kill the old chief, moved to the Manambolo River where her descendants still live on the riverbanks and are known as Vazimba Ampelamana. The descendants of the chief who sidestepped his sister's plotting moved north and became known as Beosy.

In the *tsingy* the Vazimba lived in small groups without allegiance to any overlord. During the colonial period the French army tried to capture Vazimba, Beosy and others to make them live a sedentary and controllable life in villages. This was a time when many Vazimba went into hiding under the *tsingy* and there could be no better place to get lost.

The French colonel in charge of pacifying the region was called Valdi. He made a military camp at Tsiandro, and the cultivation of rice, tilled by Vazimba prisoners, was introduced to feed his soldiers. One day on patrol Colonel Valdi was captured by a notorious bandit Marombala, who kept him as a slave for herding cattle. He could not run away since he did not know which way to go. But over the years of seasonal grazing rounds he scattered written messages calling for rescue with impunity since his captors could not read. He was finally rescued, but refused to allow the army to kill his bandit captors, and some gratefully returned with him to Tsiandro to help stabilise the region. Among the good things said of Valdi is that he planted the first mango trees in the west. By the end of the colonial period many Vazimba had left the *tsingy* to return to their herds in the savannah.

Our last camp was at Ankinajao under some splendid big kapok trees. The air rained with their seeds as a flock of parakeets spent until sunset feeding. Owls hooted as night fell. Screech owls are particularly feared because they bring messages of looming disaster from the dead. And they befriend witches. It is said that when witches dance on the tombs, the owls are with them. Speaking for myself, I love the night's noises, I feel safe in my sleeping bag, and when I wake up and can't think where I am, I listen to the night while I try to remember.

13

Bekopaka, when we returned, was noisy all night because an important Antandroy man had just died. According to custom his whole herd of cattle was in the process of being slaughtered. His children would not inherit any of his herd. His body would remain unburied, for weeks if necessary, until all the cattle were dead. The problem was that other festivities were approaching and unless the body had been buried the town could not celebrate. A lot of pressure was put on the Antandroy family to hurry up and get him buried in time.

Next morning, while all this was going on, I started looking for a form of transport, but there was nothing except two-wheeled carts pulled by zebu. Ibrahim's jeep was stuck the other side of the Manambolo River, and the Project had a four-wheel drive but it was based in Antsalova, two days away by foot or cart. Not that the roads were more than glorified cart tracks.

So it was by zebu cart that I travelled to Soalala village; setting off in the pre-dawn cold, I wrapped myself in my sleeping bag. Carts are always uncomfortable but I arranged baggage knowing I was in for a long day. At least I had the cart to myself, with a young Sakalava charioteer.

Dawn sent red streaks across the sky. The zebu didn't mind going fast in the cool hours and they trotted well. The fat sturdy humps on their backs showed them to be in peak condition and whenever we hit a downhill stretch they broke into a canter. 'Ati, ati,' the lad encouraged them. After an hour the track took us down into the wide sandy bed of the Manambolo River, along the riverbed sandbanks and splashing through the channels between them.

A pale mist was suspended over the water, and the sandbanks poking up through it caught the first rays of sun. The zebus' feet were stepping into pools of mist.

A fierce haul up the riverside brought us back into forest, wet dew dripped off overhead branches as the early sun made the canopy begin to steam, and the light picked out beads of dew along giant spider webs.

My purpose was to go west by zebu to Soatana, thence on foot until I reached a series of three lakes where I would inflate my canoe, paddle out on to the middle lake, named Somalip, and head south until I found the camp of Richard Lewis, an Englishman working on research into the nesting habits of Madagascar fish eagles. He said it was paradise, but I'd need a canoe; I couldn't imagine he had many visitors, and I looked forward to spending some days watching him at work. Meanwhile here, the forest birds were all after early worms for breakfast.

Passing through villages and hamlets the zebu sensed food and gave trouble, obstinately trying to veer off the road, aiming straight for women who sat sifting rice, or trying to push piglets out of their feed troughs. They galloped towards one trough with such determination the pigs scattered and the trough was overturned. When not terrorising piglets in this way, cattle are used for tilling the fields after the rice harvest when the paddies are flooded and the zebu are attached to pronged wooden ploughs to break up and turn over the mud.

Cattle represent more than wealth; the continuity and wellbeing of the herd is seen to parallel that of the clan and the cattle's association with the ancestors is shown in their sacrificial use. They are not sold unless someone is very ill, in which case they could be sold to buy medicine or just as likely sacrificed to appease the cause of malady.

As I had begun to discover at the New Year Ceremony, the colouring of one's cattle produces their destiny: those with white muzzles, as if wearing nosebags, are believed to be restricted in development. They represent dead capital and their owner will not prosper through them. Dappled cattle will cause property and riches constantly to change hands, bringing uncertainty, while cattle of one colour betoken solidarity. However, pure black zebu bring ruin, like black fields devastated by locust swarms, but black and white zebu, like those yoked to our cart, are considered safe.

This did not prevent us having a crash, cantering down a slope to get up speed to climb the steep bank ahead. The cart bounced so high that the shaft pole shot up in front and the harness broke, leaving one zebu free. The driver quickly handed me the reins and caught the loose beast.

Sometimes at a walk the lad dozed, his legs outstretched on the shaft, it seemed he had gone to sleep but every now and then he would twitch one of the zebu's tails to keep them moving. We stopped for three hours in midday heat, unhitched the beasts and watered them in the river. After a lunch of rice and corned beef I fell asleep in the shade of a tree.

The zebu moved slowly after the break, it was still hot and we ploughed through tall grasses feather-headed at four metres, which bowed under the yoke. The savannah was dotted with palm trees, dom palms with reddish inedible fruits, and others which were being tapped for palm wine.

Dried up lakebeds made jarring travel, a marsh churned when still wet by zebu browsing and searching for fodder among the lotus flowers. When I asked the lad his age he said he was born in Alahamady, the first day, which gives a cattlehorn destiny. Its image is a bull rooting up the earth. I thought of our lines 'Monday's child is fair of face; Tuesday's . . . full of grace; Wednesday, full of woe; Thursday's child (that's me) has far to go.' Perhaps it all came down to *vintana*. Mine was certainly holding true.

One of the very few pleasures of zebu-cart travel is being able to hear the enormous amount of birdsong and having time to spot the soloists and the choirs. In Malagasy folklore there are birds of fortune and birds of ill-omen. The bringers of bad luck are types of tufted umbrette and crested kingfisher whose name *vitsy* means few and, being a solitary bird without a social flock, it foretells a state of few friends, little family and general misery. Birds of fortune like larks, warblers, some sparrows and snipes are believed to have saved people's lives by alerting them to danger, so it became *fady* to eat such birds. The kestrel, *hitsikitsika*, lives alongside people in villages, nesting under their hut eaves, and serves the community by catching mice and rats. It even fights off kites which overfly villages to seize chicks. The *fady* protecting the kestrel says rather fiercely that anyone who kills it will be cursed with abnormal children, beaten by their foes and outcast. Also it is *fady* to destroy the nests of big birds, since they symbolise the family house and to break a carefully built nest may destroy your own home. The white egret is the servant of cattle herdsmen. It stays with the herd to eat the leeches and flies that pester the zebu, and when the lads are searching for the herd in tall grasslands they can find them by sighting the egrets.

Among the legendary birds of Madagascar is the Kokolampy, a huge bird with long beak and, according to the legend, if you see the bird you will die. My logical friend Moïse Ramilamintsoa said it is a real bird and once, while he was camping at dusk, a local army officer insisted he stay at his house because the Kokolampy frequently visited the area at night. He would already have spotted Moïse, so he would be coming for him. And sure enough with a noisy scrabbling something heavy landed on the tin roof. Not giant, but big enough, Moïse said, and in the neighbourhood they claimed it had killed people and cattle.

We came up against a huge herd of cattle being driven in the opposite direction and had to plunge into the bushes to avoid them. The lad thrust the reins to me and jumped down with a stick to stop his pair getting unruly. They don't look dangerous because their horns are beautifully bowed. Nicely bowed horns are a hallmark of quality, and often the horns nearly meet in a circle. I wished my highland cattle in Britain had safe horns like these. Mine have a span of a metre, curving out and forward, and they are lethal. It is my job to keep my cattle tame enough to handle but wild enough to fear humans; when you are charged by horned cattle trying to be friendly it can be frightening.

The great cattle herdsmen here are Antandroy; we passed a group of their tombs and stopped to walk around. The largest tomb was like a decent-sized house with a corrugated tin roof and roofed verandah all the way round the building.

The exterior walls were painted with murals, one showing a crocodile catching a man by his leg and pulling him upsidedown. Numerous cattle were depicted with mega-sized humps, and the east wall had a mirror set in it. The lad told me 300 head of zebu were sacrificed and eaten at the most recent burial here; the tomb was still in use. Others in the area were smaller and had model houses on top. In contrast, the living families made do with poor grass thatched huts.

Later we met a zebu-cart overflowing with festive passengers dressed in fresh clean *lambas*. Five children were with them, also five bottles of rum, a cassette player and some slabs of raw meat. They were on their way to their mother's village for a ceremony to do with children. Their father had killed a zebu for the event; if he did not make this sacrifice, the children would not belong to him by right. They belong to the mother until that sacrifice. To affiliate the child into the male lineage, the father of the mother invokes the ancestors. The festival is called Tarikosy to Beosy and Soran'anake to Sakalava. A man can affiliate several children together since one zebu per child is far too expensive nowadays.

At the end of the day we reached my destination Soatana and I found a night's lodgings with a lady shopkeeper. She said I could sleep in the storeroom, which was also the foam mattress store, so the big bed was heaped high.

I climbed up to get on to it promising myself a really comfortable night until, lying back, I saw the ceiling was covered in hornets' nests, dozens of them. In case they were active, I decided to put up my mosquito net.

I had inflated the canoe on the lakeshore but wasn't sure which of the lakes it was; only two were visible not three. So I aimed straight out towards the middle of the big lake, the paddling felt good and a cool breeze helped me along.

There seemed to be no fishing villages on the shores and no signs of habitation, though in the lake to the east some fishermen in pirogues were banging their canoe-sides with bits of wood and smacking their paddles flat on the water to frighten a shoal of fish into their nets.

Mid-lake I remembered my leaks and expected them to make themselves known, as the canoe was carrying maximum heavyweight baggage with my backpack wrapped in a black plastic sack and my fragile equipment in a waterproof kayak-bag, with a basket of food propped behind me. No apparent leaks. Could that mean I had reached Paradise?

After an hour, when I was beginning to think I was lost, I

spotted the white front of a tent on the shore. Success! Because it was Sunday, the full team of Richard, plus his three Malagasy co-workers, were in camp. Trees were not climbed and fish eagles' chicks not weighed and measured, apparently, on Sundays. But I discovered they were expecting a more important visitor than me.

It was the opening of the fishing season and the elder whose job it was to preside over the ceremonial involved was coming to lunch. While we awaited his arrival the team told me about the different characters of each lake. This one, Somalip, is joined to the one in the west by a small channel and they have a seasonal link to the Manambolo River; the lake to the east is separate, narrower, deeper and foreboding. Fishermen said their lines can touch bottom in the linked lakes but the third, Ankierke, is too deep to fathom. 'How deep?' I asked. 'Oh no, you can't ask that,' Richard put in, 'because none of them can count.' This spooky place was where the elder's village was located. It has a bad reputation for crocodiles and in the past they used to be so numerous they killed someone every week. Perhaps this is why there are so few villages. But nowadays the croc numbers are being decimated by poachers after their skins.

The elder eventually arrived, without ceremony, and we sat down to an excellent lunch of roasted tilapia, caught that morning beside the camp. He explained to me that you can still go out to fish in the closed season, as I had seen en route, with nets and canoes, it is the use of the *couhou* the elders have banned. The *couhou* is made of wood, like a plunger, with a solid square base, and can stun whole shoals of fish. By tradition it was also forbidden to use a net with holes smaller than four fingers' width.

The elder said as soon as he opens the season lots of people turn up to catch all the fish they can for marketing in their home villages, fishing day and night until end of season. The local people don't like it but their rules of hospitality towards fellow-Sakalava instruct them to make the guests welcome and let them hire nets and canoes. I suggested he resolve the problem by raising the price of hire, but he said he could not.

As for the ritual opening, though the state hunting and fishing season was already open, the traditional one was waiting for the right astrological *vintana*. He thought this week on Wednesday or Thursday, but feared that Wednesday being 'the day of poor return' might bring a poor season of fish; and Thursday could be troublesome. Thursday's name is Alakamisy and *misy* means 'there is', implying that all one's needs in life will be met. But it also has a negative side as a day of slaves, a black and weak day, and is generally considered dangerous for work but acceptable for most sacred rites except burial. The wrong choice of day could herald a poor season. It can be hard to avoid life's unseen pitfalls and traps. I was told a fishy proverb: 'The fish which swims against the current learns to master the current,' meaning he must align himself and make the right decisions to arrive upstream, and by achieving this and reaching a pool he is greater in spirit than the fishes living there. 'And when he descends the river, he becomes master of all.'

Richard explained the problems of working with Sakalava who strongly resist any idea that comes from outside, mistrusting the Malagasy plateau tribes as much as the foreigners. They want no form of interference and offered benefits are seen as a trap. Despite the work being frustratingly slow and often unsuccessful, each one of the team felt the place was a paradise.

'Of course it's paradise, it's a pristine wetland, crystal clear water, almost original forest, in perfect condition, what more could you ask?'

'In paradise you'd find everything you needed: water, fish, birds, animals and the forest. There are many lakes but none of them are in such an untouched condition.'

'Perhaps it's paradise by default, there's no other candidates, and we are lucky to be here now. Our grandchildren won't see this, this will be gone in twenty years; people will come and make villages, cut the forest, hunt the wildlife.

'And now is the right season to be here, it heats up to 35–40°c in the rainy season, very humid and thick with mosquitoes and millions of other biting insects. There are even insects that bite the crocodiles. This time of year is the best.'

Despite that assurance, as darkness fell there was a ferocious onslaught of mosquitoes, but the team slapped their bare legs in an unconcerned way, hardly noticing, and after an hour the mossies had almost disappeared. As we talked, two brown lemurs sidled into the supply tent, their tails held aloft like cats with a plume a half-metre long. They only steal ripe fruit, and the branch of bananas was safe because it was still green. The lemurs were playful but, the team said, they never stole things. They may pick up your pen or notes, but they never take them away.

Monday morning means off to work, even in Paradise, and Richard and his Malagasy team member, Lukman, planned to show me their work checking two fish eagle nest sites, the second being in a typically majestic baobab tree. Somewhat without thinking I asked if they would let me climb the baobab, too. I knew that I might never get another chance to do so.

At seven a.m. we set off paddling across the lake. The team had Sevylor inflatable canoes like mine, but a two-man version. It was quite a surprise to find my ugly duckling was not alone in the world. Richard was delighted by the smaller version and asked to paddle it on the way back. The small ones are sadly no longer on the market, being discontinued about the time I bought mine ten years ago.

On the far shore we portaged the canoes across a forested arm of land to the next lake, then paddled to the far side of that to visit an active nest. We disturbed a treeful of fruit bats on the way, which took to the air as a flock and wheeled in a massive circle over the treetops with a thousand squeaking cries.

The first tree for Richard to climb was a tamarind, unclimbed since last year. Richard picked the thinner of two vines that hung from the tree, saying that if it broke he would try the thicker one. I was still trying to work out the logic of this as he swung up into the lowest branches, nicely spaced for climbing. Fish eagle nests are always at the very top of a tree so the bird gets the best vantage, the eagle's eye view. Crying her anger, the female fish eagle lifted off the nest and winged around above the tree. From below with me, Lukman identified three birds flying around us – the mother, father, and a youngster from last year. Fragments of bark rained down as Richard moved out to the nest.

His job up there was to weigh, measure and mark the two eggs, since only one chick would survive. The chicks are born a couple of days apart which makes a difference to their size, and they are naturally so aggressive the larger chick bullies the other and pushes it away from any food. So the difference in size escalates and within ten days the smaller chick is usually dead.

'Is it the survival of the fittest?' I asked.

'We can't say if only one chick is meant to survive. Last year we removed the second chick from a nest and reared it until the end of the most aggressive stage, then put it back and the two grew up all right together. The parents provided enough food for both. But psychologically both chicks can't live together as youngsters.'

We paddled back across the middle lake to reach the baobab tree, which had had an active nest the year before but now there only seemed to be one bird. Having been to the nest once before they had left a guide line hanging in place, so we attached a rope to the line and hoisted it up.

The nest was high above the forest canopy, but I still wanted to go up there. This was my tree. At its base the circumference was equal to a circle of ten people with arms outstretched, and then the trunk went up sheer and smooth, not splaying into branches until the top. Very much the tree that God planted upsidedown.

Richard wondered if I wanted to change my mind, warning me, 'There's nothing to hold on to, not even a fingerhold. The trunk is greasy and slippery. It flakes away in your hands, so don't expect any help from it. And never put your weight on branches, the chances are they'll break. They're not like solid wood, they're fleshy and feeble, so even if a branch looks fat it may break under you. Just make sure, if you've got to sit on a branch, that is's a damned fat one.'

He had brought a second harness and showed me how to stick my legs through the legholes, and double the strap back through the buckles to be sure. Then he clipped some steel karabiners on to my belt. He was patient and thorough. The equipment was not mountaineering gear, it was speleo stuff for caving; the elastic quality of mountain ropes makes them less suitable for trees.

Richard went up ahead of me, then I was ready. Lukman clipped my ascender gadget to the rope. Pull the ascender clip up and push down with your foot in its rope sling, and up you go. I had to keep repeating the instructions in case I forgot them. The rope looked very thin; at 9 mm it was spindly. After some small confusions at three metres above ground I got the hang of it, the ratchet whirred with each step, the longer the step the less the effort; it felt like climbing the side of a skyscraper, all I could see of my tree was the grey bark shooting off into the sky.

The rope led me up through the branches of other trees, slowly up through the forest canopy until my head came out above the leaves. The rope spun and I began to feel vulnerable. To get on to the fork of branches above me was tricksy because the rope lay tight against the wood, held by my weight. My chin was level with a branch but the rest of my body was hanging in space, there was no way I could pull myself up on to the branch from below.

'Find the sling with your foot, use it to push yourself up, and here's a second loop above it. You must get off the rope now and transfer your weight on to the slings.'

These are not simple manoeuvres when you are dangling in the air with your heart hammering in fear, but once I'd managed to get into the fork of branches I began to relax. The view was commanding, we could see both ends of one lake and everything that was going on. Some fishermen paddling canoes, a bunch of wild cattle grazing a grassy shore, some lemurs moving between trees, but all that was in the world below us. For us on top of the canopy the other hemisphere was sky, the realm of birds.

The fish eagles' courtship display takes place in the air at the stage when the two birds are not quite sure of each other; both birds fly up high but one goes higher then swoops and dives down as if to attack the lower. At the last instant the lower bird flips over on its back and presents its talons. The upper eagle also extends its talons and the two birds lock feet together and they tumble down through the sky in a cartwheel motion, breaking up again just before nearing ground.

The female eagle was perched nearby now, watching us. Richard was puzzled why there was no pair here, as last year. He checked the nest but found no eggs. 'It's worrying if they don't breed, this Madagascar fish eagle is in the top five rarest birds of prey in the world. We estimate there are only fifty to a hundred pairs in existence and they all live in Madagascar. On these three lakes where we're based there are ten pairs, that means ten to twenty per cent of the world population is right here.'

The nest itself was enormous, about a metre across, still above me at the top of the highest and thinnest branches. They started to wobble as Richard went up them. 'It's always scary when it wobbles. The further I go the worse it gets. You've got to decide whether the branch will hold you all the way out to the nest. I've been to a few nests that I'll never re-visit they're so dangerous. Trouble is, you get so close, thinking I've come all this way, I'm not going down without checking. Even when you can touch the nest you can't see into it because it's above you. Sometimes I have to climb up the side of the nest, fingers crossed that it's well built. Then when I manage to get on to the nest, if there's a chick there, it's usually trying to sink its talons in me, while I'm trying to put it into a sack to weigh it, or ring it.'

As jobs went, this took some beating. I wasn't going to compete to look inside an empty nest. In fact my mind was already frozen with panic at how I was going to get down the tree. I needed to slide over the side of the branch, find the slings with my feet and learn to use the descender. As I moved out into space seeking the slings with my toes, I was in fact shaking. Trying to turn around on the sling to face the trunk was no fun either, but all was accomplished without mishap and in five minutes I had reached the ground.

In the late afternoon I went for a bath in a secluded bay and on the way back I heard plaintive cawing from a leafy tree. A young female fish eagle was sitting there, trying to sound appealing. Back at camp Richard sighed and told me that was Luva. Her wing had been smashed a year ago when her nest was blown out of its tree. The team looked after her but, because of multiple fractures to the wing, Luva was sent all the way to Nairobi for an operation. The wing was mended and she was able to fly, but the plan to release her backfired. She had grown used to people giving her fish to eat, and her time in captivity had taught her not to fear humans, so whenever she saw someone carrying a fish she swooped down to grab it.

'She has no manners. So we've brought her back to where she was born to teach her to survive but to leave people alone. She's angry because I wave big cloths if she swoops at me, I'm not feeding her much, in order to force her to hunt for herself. Sadly, when she does try to hunt, having no established territory, she gets attacked by the other fish eagles.'

In fact, I had heard Luva's story earlier from Toro on the Manambolo River. He had been mystified why people hadn't simply eaten the bird with the broken wing, instead of spending big money on repairs. Perhaps he was right.

On my final day I went with Lukman to spook lake. A fairly large crocodile had left fresh prints where we put the canoe in the water and other croc activity was evident around the shore. We could see the island where the elder said a mermaid lived. He had seen only the torso of a woman with long dark hair. The villagers said she had the lower body of a fish but, like all mermaids, she fled when approached.

My return journey from Soatana began with a night ride by zebu cart filled with freshly cut hay. We left at sunset and, being cool, the oxen rattled along at a canter. The moon was rising, almost a full moon, and every now and then a bat's wings flitted across it in sinister silhouette. My purpose was to return to Bekopaka in time for the ceremonial inauguration of a new water well, due to take place on the morrow.

14

Early morning in Bekopaka: I revived myself with hot coffee and fresh honeycomb on rice-bread at a market stall, as I read through a poster of the week's programme of events leading up to the celebration of Independence Day on the following weekend. Today's inauguration of four new wells would mark the start of festivities.

In town for the inauguration were a UN project group from Antsalova, who offered me a lift midweek back up north with them for the continuation of celebrations. I welcomed the chance of revisiting Antsalova. The project had been responsible for creating these new wells, supplying the materials and technical knowledge, while the local people did the digging.

At the scheduled start of proceedings at eight a.m., the only person at the town flagpole was me. At nine a.m. there was slight action when the zebu for sacrifice was led to a nearby tree. Finally, from a lower avenue came a group playing flutes and drums. The music called out to people come and join us, and from all sides a procession formed behind them.

At the raising of the flag the schoolchildren lined up for the singing of the national anthem with gusto and pride. The zebu was led over and symbolically cleansed, laid on its left side in front of the flagpole. After the invocation and the sacrifice, and during the skinning and cutting of the meat, we had the speeches. The new Deputy of the region gave a very long speech to update people on his plans for the next twelve months. He mentioned that within about a year the Reserve would change status to National Park. To me, this had enormous implications but I was still working on my opinions about it.

The crowd formed a procession led by the flutes and drums and walked dancing, clapping and chanting, to each of the four wells in turn; at each the elder spoke the words of wellbeing and, using a leafy twig, splashed blood on to the well-mouth.

The inauguration ended at noon, by which time it was hot and dusty and I was happy when Haja invited me to join their cocktail party for the Bekopaka elders. There was Pepsi, beer and Fanta and they had even managed to find enough glasses. My party ice-breaking technique was to show the twenty-five elders a photo of my cattle and dogs in England. This would help them place my status! Then Vongy, the project leader from Antsalova, took up his guitar and the complete Malagasy project team gave a concert in close harmony. After that Vongy sang a duet with the President of the region, whose voice was soft, melodious and well-trained, and quite a surprise coming from a middle-aged man with thick spectacles. In fact he had a long musical background, as had Vongy who was a renowned jazz player. Some form of music is a part of most Malagasy men's lives and male harmony singing is always a pleasure to hear.

A 'Grand Ball' was being held that evening in the school class-room, entrance fee 500 fmg (10p). Two young friends came to see me, saying they couldn't go to the Ball because they didn't have enough money to pay the entrance. Two such Prince Charmings had to be helped to go and find their Cinderellas, so we all went. I danced with various men; one only came up to my shoulder but he did an excellent rumba. Many dances are performed in lines, men opposite women, or in couples like the basic Gay Gordons routine, circling and occasionally reversing. I left quite early while everyone was still behaving with dignity.

The next day a young man declared his love for me over some frothing buckets of palm wine which was probably very potent. I told him I was appallingly lazy and would never do any cooking or housework, nor work in his rice-fields. He stopped pestering me straight away.

The team from Antsalova had come to Bekopaka in the Project's four-wheel drive, so we went back together, though not exactly in comfort, as the roads were some of the worst I had ever experienced. The direct route being impassable, since all bridges were broken, we took a long loop to the west. The driver had pushed aside a couple of fallen trees on his way south, but we still had to stop and clear bits of road. At Antsalova they gave me the use of a spare room at the project bungalow while the

Independence celebrations continued. The events of the next day included the traditional Sakalava sport of *moraingy*, where two opponents beat the hell out of each other with arms and bare fists until one steps back. Any retreat or submission and the fight is over.

The tomtoms beat hard as the youths strutted cockily in the ring, giving yelping wow-yow cries and making insulting gestures to potential challengers. Incongruously, some wore tall beehive hats of woven straw with small brims. They were all bare-chested, with belted *lambas* round their hips. To avoid family feuds, sons of the same parents are not allowed to fight each other.

The first battle was between a stocky youth and a wiry one who fisted his way to victory in a matter of seconds. A bout between two other lads lasted nearly a minute, and another was over before it had started, as one contestant backed before being hit. Losing that way made him so angry he stalked around the ring trying to pick a new fight. He found one and lost again. A foxy-faced lad in a pink and orange striped *lamba* won the next round, using his head as well. How ferocious their faces could seem in the ring, yet a moment later they were relaxed into soft sweet smiles. Physical damage is very rare and the sport is a great crowd-puller. Usually the *moraingy* takes place on feast days or market days because of its spectator appeal.

In the countryside the build-up to the festivities had been intense. Women were preparing extra food for family feasts, one lady stopped to show me her basketful of bats, black furry skin on their backs and great black skin wings with a span of half a metre. She was selling them for 1000 fmg (20p) each.

Also in the villages there were long hair-dressing sessions. Apart from the typical Sakalava knobs, some had up to twenty plaits knotted and joined in different ways, the best had four plaits aside of descending thickness, rolled and looped in a wave each side. Hairstyles can denote joy or sorrow; animal-fat is used to grease the hair when plaiting it for a feast. While for some women in mourning many little plaits are prohibited, they must let their hair hang down untidily and uncombed. In some places people cut their hair after a death in the family. But now the mood was festive. Children ran around in high spirits. If you are a foreigner you can't help noticing the large number of children in the villages because they are all following you.

Fifty per cent of the population of Madagascar is under fifteen years old. I could believe it! The demographic growth rate is among the highest in the world and the population will double within twenty years. What will be left of the countryside for the children and their children? And who cares? The Malagasy folk believe that children are a gift from God and must not be refused (for example by birth control) and the more offspring you have the more you are blessed.

In urban areas the problem is understood. It is, as always, the rural areas that so urgently need first step education towards family planning. There are organisations with clinics in accessible areas, but they have not been able to reach the grass roots level. I was already at work on raising international funding for a radio drama series for rural education on family planning. To be acceptable it would have to be performed in Malagasy and somehow come from within their culture.

After dark on the eve of Independence Day the children of Antsalova had a lantern procession. Scores of tinies carrying tall candles and paper lanterns with candles glowing in them, paraded around the dusty streets. It was an ethereal sight. Then the evening began in earnest with firecrackers and young men loosing home-made fireballs out of Pepsi bottles, and there was a big night market with candle-lit stalls selling kebabs, roasted peanuts, and dishes heaped with local specialities. Later there was a dance, and again I did the polka and waltzed with much pleasure, even if towering over my partners.

Independence Day itself began with the lethargy of a morning after the night before. There were awnings and flags over the VIP box for the Deputy and President of region. When the townsfolk finally appeared, it was in full finery with fluorescent colours and sun umbrellas. The regional President who had sung so nicely in Bekopaka, inspected the line-up of gendarmes. The day seemed to roll past. Musicians with old wooden instruments played traditional songs in the afternoon and modern ones after dark, using the distorting speaker system for amplification. For dinner with the UN team, we had each made or bought something special to share at the table; the prize went to a girl teacher from Tsiandro for raiding her hen for enough eggs to make a meringue pie.

The team was a credit to the UN project, and during my stay I noted their work to take local pressure off the *tsingy* by promoting better use of natural resources and new sources of income. The introduction of ducks and rabbits had been fairly successful; there were twenty rabbits now in villages, and bee-keeping had also been encouraged. Tree nurseries had continual problems with cattle breaking in and with insect attacks. This year the project would try putting nurseries under local supervision.

They also planned to get a botanical inventory of the region made, to include medicinal plants, essential oils, and their uses. Twenty essential-oil plants had already been identified. Reforesting against erosion was primarily being supported by schoolchildren and football teams in a bid to promote young people's awareness of the environment before they grew up to be distrustful suspicious adults.

Since its beginning the project had initiated two village pharmacies, giving them credit at first, then selling them supplies, and both were now autonomous. Vaccination programmes were happening to improve livestock, and they were trying to motivate people to send their children to school. This was all a prelude to the future creation of a national park in the region promised by the Deputy.

From all I heard and saw of eco-tourism, I still wondered how it could effectively bring economic development to the region it was intended to serve. Certainly some women could make and sell artefacts and some men could be porters. But was that it? Perhaps the future tourists would fly to Bekopaka and drive to the *tsingy*. I was in favour of keeping access difficult. Travel by zebu-cart, as I had done, would put people in touch with nature before arriving far better than a new road. If something is too easy, it is relatively meaningless.

Unintentional night outings had become a feature of this month in the mid-west, whether trying to find ways out of the *tsingy* and back to my camp or stumbling through dark forest thankful for the lack of dense undergrowth, following dry stream beds that turned wet and muddy with fine silt that sank me to my knees. Such night walks were usually my own fault having strayed too far without noticing the time, forgetting that the days were growing shorter. Going to Antsingy forest, east of Antsalova, I simply set out too late to arrive before dark.

As the sun set we hastened our steps across the cattle grasslands, seeing the forest still twelve kilometres away. There were small villages but we didn't stop longer than to exchange greetings. My companions were a guide called Honoré and a skinny porter who couldn't speak French but was always cheerful and skipped along carrying my heavy pack at a great speed. A poor path was marked on my map as a road, but it was certainly impassable, and finally invisible. The full moon rose as we marched in single file through grasses that rose over our heads.

Two hours later inside the forest, blackness prevailed, and we lost our way in a thicket. Twice the guide stopped with a jolt and used his machete to cut away webs with big spiders lying in wait for unsuspecting victims. Their bites are painful for six to eight hours, very occasionally fatal.

Our general stumblings also woke a troupe of fulvis lemurs which vocalised their alarm, the call spreading from tree to tree. Holes in other trees housed lepilemurs, one we saw was Rificodatus a nocturnal grey leaf-eating lepilemur. Tired enough to camp where we stood, we persevered until we reached a river with a small cascade.

At dawn I found we had camped in an extraordinarily pretty place among small outcrops of *tsingy* where a stream poured through an arch of rock, so I stopped there for a day to see where I was. These are not humid jungle forests, they are dry, deciduous, and heaven for botanists. In our rambles Honoré showed me a multitude of plants and said no British botanist has yet visited the place. The 1990 survey report had also bemoaned the lack of a botanist in their team.

Gurgling noises led to where parts of streams vanished down into the rocks, with springs and low fountains surging up nearby, only to disappear equally suddenly. One beautiful stream had carved a bed on *tsingy* with rock spires poking up from the water's depths, another wound between banks of blue forget-me-nots on scalloped stream terraces. An hour to the north we came to more *tsingy* with a roof we could walk on. It had deep narrow crevasses and a stream winding through a temple-shape of a great pointed archway with vaulted stone arch above.

Night walks whetted my appetite for greater things, and back in Antsalova I studied my maps.

15

Having crossed the *tsingy* from west to east near Bekopaka, I wanted to find out if I could recross the central part of the *tsingy* barrier near Antsalova. Way back, when I first applied for a permit, I had proposed following the Beboka River through, and near Antsalova where the river flowed out across the plain, I noted it had enough water to be feasible by canoe. The Project vehicle was due to take two teachers back to Tsiandro primary school on the other side of the *tsingy* the day after the Indepedence Day celebrations, so I arranged to have a lift with them.

It was not possible to find a guide who knew the river canyon. No one knew it, except hunters and honey-gatherers living in the forest. But I met the old guide for the survey teams, now retired, and he appointed as my guide the eldest of his fifteen children, who turned out to be Honoré with whom I had already travelled, supported by his friend Emil as porter, since it was likely that I would be defeated and have to walk out carrying all my gear. The plan was that while I negotiated the river in my canoe, they would make their way on foot along the riverbanks where possible, and where it wasn't, pile the baggage into the canoe and swim for it. The length of the trip was not known, nor the obstacles; we guessed at four days.

Where we started it was a small river and it changed direction with every rock ledge, the sedimentary formations giving horizontal layers scooped out by the current. One soft clay layer was turquoise blue and it gave its colour to the water. As the river dropped down the ledges in the rock it became a chain of lakes when it flowed through long smooth open fissures.

A bushfire had started away to the north and was fanned down to the river. The air was thick with pale smoke and raining grass ash. Through it I could see a dozen kites and other birds of prey circling on the hot air hunting for small fleeing animals.

I was not too worried Honoré and Emil had walked ahead with the baggage and I knew I would find them in due course. As for me, the river gave enough protection, though shallow here and studded with rocks, and the roar of crackling grass fires is always deceptively loud. But it was impressive to see sheets of fire jumping and great fireballs leaping into the sky, letting go of the land and hurtling upwards as each gust of wind brought fresh bursts of life to the wall of flames.

More relevant to me was a different roar, of water from rapids ahead. I nudged the canoe into an inlet and went to take a look. The noise was a four-metre cascade in a mass of rocks that I would have to portage around. I wanted to see round the next bend as well, which meant walking across the cascade. I calculated I could jump on stepping stones across the lip at the top of the falls but in the middle the gaps were too large and I was forced to brace myself against the not too strong current and use some slippery underwater rocks.

Turning the corner I found the canyon rose up into a cliff spectacularly striped orange, black, white and yellow. The stripy effect was adorned with stalactites of calcium on roots of plants, one central bunch of roots was coated in frilly pink and black trailing shapes. It was like a backdrop to a theatre, with a stage of flat sandstone, and rock tiers and overhangs making a broad staircase descending to a sandy cove where the cascade fell into a deep turquoise pool.

The pool was fabulous to paddle on, about three metres deep and the water so clear it was transparent. Over it dashed scarlet dragonflies and blue and orange kingfishers, and I thought I glimpsed a turtle. I was also reassured to see Honoré on the bank. It was midday and he told me we were close to the hamlet of Betrakaka so we walked there.

It was a small rather deserted group of huts, low to the ground, I could not have stood upright in them, thatched with dry grass, walls of straw or of lightly woven sticks and mud, with a shady overhang or roof held up by poles. Just the old and a few young people remained. I told them I was English from Britain and asked them who they were. An old man replied they were mostly Beosy (sometimes spelled Beosh), mixed with some Sakalava and others. More men arrived with daggers at their belts and an odd spear or spade, and I was invited into one of the tiny huts. We sat on floor mats and a bowl of yams came from an even tinier kitchen alongside, but it was a big bowl. Beosy, though not pygmy, have a different physiognomy from the Sakalava, with longish frizzy hair, red-tinged at the front. Few of the Sakalava could understand their language or dialect. This was savannah, cattle country, with well fenced stockades, a pretty region of conical hills with outcrops of limestone. Not yet much trace of the *tsingy* ahead. The river was in a low canyon, every bend had caves in the cliffs many with stalactites coated in dry velvet moss. I troddled along trying to follow narrow waterways as the river broke into rocky shallows; I was adopting a kneeling technique to enable me to see what lay ahead. My canoe grew softer by the hour but I couldn't be bothered to stop and pump it up.

Just above waterlevel I noticed a group of giants' cauldrons, which are uniformly circular hollows in the rock, enlarged by the action of stones inside them being rolled around the cavity by the water's force when the river is in spate. I wondered how many years or hundreds of years would pass before those stones become pebbles.

We camped on a sandbank, an early night in preparation for the day ahead.

On Day Two we did six hours downriver. There was a sensational spot where a twenty-metre chute of water poured down a mammoth slab of smooth rock into a vertical-sided fault between flat rock borders, making a deep narrow blue lake. I threw my canoe over the edge and picked my way down behind it, carrying my small daily rucksack. After it I canoed through some breathtakingly lovely pools with a number of fresh-water turtles and metre-long eels in them.

Waterfalls were often considered sacred and dangerous on account of the spirits that dwelt there. They were favoured places for witch-doctors to sit and meditate. They particularly liked to sit under the curtain formed by the sheet of falling water. When falling water sparkled in the sun, it was believed to be a sure sign of the supernatural power of the place.

There was no sign of my lads, perhaps they had taken another way, and in fact I seldom saw them all day, which occasionally worried me since they carried the food and camping gear. Fortunately, they found me at lunchtime and we stopped to brew rice on the flat rocks where the river broadened into a series of pools. While we ate a fossa came down to drink at a pool. The size of a fox, it was unaware of us and gave itself a quick grooming before stalking off.

The afternoon was again glorious with many more giants' cauldrons, but the shallows where the river divided among numerous islands were only just canoeable, needing many porterages and I was glad my canoe was so light I could carry it under one arm. It was probably not a totally runnable river at any time of year, for in the rainy season it would be a wild torrent of cascades.

I met up with the lads at an impassable barricade of rocks and deep channels and we used the canoe to ferry first the baggage then the boys. They thought it was great sport.

That night we camped on a rock shelf which backed into a cave. At the front a useful channel of water ran past the camp. The tragedy of the river was that, as I saw with more and more certainty, it carried the disease bilharzia. The carrier snails were everywhere and breeding. For myself, it was too late to avert the threat. It is said you will be all right if your skin has no cuts, and you avoid the shallows, but after the *tsingy* my feet and legs were covered in cuts and sores. Thank God for modern medicine; the disease used to be incurable. In fact I had caught it fifteen years ago in West Africa, but lightly and I hoped that, like a vaccination, it would give me immunity this time.

I had my first dunking when I tipped over while shooting a small cascade I hadn't meant to tackle. The canoe flipped upsidedown. Everything floated, but I had to swim quite far to catch the paddle. The next deep pool had rock teeth outcropping from the surface, smoothed by water. It felt strange to be floating over the top of *tsingy*.

As the gorge narrowed I ferried the baggage and the lads more often; swimming looked less of a good idea, for we could see crocodile sunbathing spots and their tracks leading into the water were convincing enough. The current had scooped deep pockets and caverns into the sandstone above and below the present waterlevel. Lurking shadows swam lazily and disappeared into underwater caverns and there were plenty of small fish for croc fodder flitting among the submerged needles of *tsingy*.

Honoré said that during the dry season the crocs of the Bemaraha move into the deeper caves because they don't want to be disturbed. By December there would be almost no water here. The crocodiles would live off the blind white fishes that inhabit the caves. I asked if the blind fish had eyes and he said yes, they look as if they are wearing goggles, but they can't see.

Paddling through a natural rock gateway I was immediately inside a dense *tsingy* massif, a great jumble of pinnacle rocks in a sheer-sided canyon, I pulled the canoe over some rocks and put it back into the river inside a cave which led into a short tunnel. I paddled along the tunnel and found a hole into the back of another cave which opened on to the lower river where I wanted to be. The canoe was being squeezed on both sides and the rock was slippery for my hands to push us through. Not the place for it to give up the ghost. It took two attempts before I emerged through the back of the cave out into the river.

Night Three we camped on a riverside shelf with a bed of fine white sand. It was the only possible campsite we had seen in the past hour as the gorge narrowed. I wished I knew what to expect from the canyon ahead. We were now going into the blank bit on the map and I wanted to get out forwards not backwards. It was indeed the kind of place you can't quickly walk out of. I feared it could be the worst bit of the river but hoped it would be the best. In its sheer cliffs plants fought for rootholds and lemurs skipped through the branches; it felt wonderfully wild. In a way the whole place was like heaven, because nothing about the plants and landscape was remotely familiar and my days and nights on the Beboka were like being in a parallel world. Certainly my camping places were among the most beautiful sites I had ever enjoyed. It was a phase in my travels which I realised I didn't want to end.

My second dousing happened next morning when I threw the canoe into a pool and jumped down to land in it, a jump of about one and a half metres but I missed. By late morning the riverbed became a monstrous jumble of rocks and tight vertical fissures. The extraordinary thing was how the water kept vanishing. When this happened I rammed my canoe on to the sand and went to investigate potential tunnels or channels. I was mesmerised by a whirlpool, where I parked the canoe and sat feeding things into the whirling mouth to see where they went. The best fodder was thick globs of algae that got sucked down and spun into a fine green thread, whirling down into a hole in the rocky bottom of the pool.

The remnants of the river flowed into deep cracks under a castle-sized block of *tsingy*. I followed where practical, but it was hard to know which direction was the main river, so I cut over the headland and found it again at the base of the cliffs. In fact it didn't flow out at all in this season, it went through the ground and bubbled up at the base of the cliffs.

After the cliffs the stream grew continually, joined by sources bubbling up from underground. Some were hot and smelled of sulphur. One I nearly stepped in was a loose sand hollow. I stuck the paddle down and it went in all the way, making the spring erupt into a mass of bubbles. It was time to pack up the canoe and go ahead on foot. While we were reorganising ourselves, we met some members of a funeral party washing in the river. An old Beosy-Sakalava woman had died. They said they had a day to wait before they could bury her because she died on a *fady* day. Thursday or Saturday's deaths were the easiest to bury. Four porters had carried her body to the tomb, a full day's walk. They wore white, the colour of mourning.

We were using the same path as those coming to the funeral, which meant that Honoré and Emil had to go through the whole greetings routine each time we met anyone. No matter how much they were in a hurry to get back to Antsalova, the rules of seniority applied and it would be disrespectful to rush the salutes. I had often noticed how people always said, 'May I pass?' *(Mbay ari, tompoko)* when they met on paths, and in reply the elder ones mumbled 'Yes all right'. Today's greetings were much lengthier.

Had we been going the same direction as the elders, it would be customary for my lads to carry their burdens for some way along the path.

We passed a sacred tamarind tree, where the elders would meet to decide on the posthumous name for the dead woman. The new name must not resemble the name during life. And if anyone in the village has the same name as that chosen for the deceased, the living person must change his. For it is *fady* to use the same name.

By terminating the living name at death, all links are cut and this protects the living. If you were to retain the real name, it could have dangerous consequences. The new death name must be one that pleases the dead spirit since it will be used to call up the spirit at rituals. So the families look for names which remind them of their ancestor's best qualities. Posthumous names say something definite about the dead person. Some examples are: 'He who did his duty', 'The one who was loved by a thousand', 'She who united and held together', 'The man who made work look easy', and 'He who opposed anything'. This last was not meant critically, it was more a tribute to the man's strength of independent thought.

The dead are as dependent on the living for acknowledgment as the living are dependent on the dead for blessings. The ancestor's soul can die if it is left out of the thoughts and actions of the relatives; when it gets no attention and no one cares for it, it ceases to exist. Honoré said there was a proverb 'To die once is bad enough, but to die twice is beyond bearable.'

I tried to put myself in Honoré's place. But I have never stopped to have children because I always refused to give up my freedom. My children have got to be the children of the world. To my mind couples have children to cement their marriages; my husband already had children and I don't need cement. I hoped instead that one day I would become a good elder, and a remembered ancestor.

FIVE

The Petrified Forest

16

My enthusiasm for prehistory took me north to the Mahajanga region on a search to find out what animals or monsters had lived in Madagascar before mankind arrived. Here I teamed up with the geology and palaeontology department of Mahajanga university. It felt odd to be in a big town after a month in the bush; I had to try to remember to behave like other people.

The professors were a delightful group of gentle unhurried folk, and the Dean of the Science Faculty spoke in such a soft whisper I had to ask for a summary at the end. I was fortunate to meet a seventy-year-old geologist called Eugène Razafimbelo who introduced me to his philosophy.

'In my thirty years of footwork as a geologist I sometimes feel the futility of mankind. My work will never end but man is transitory in this world, and life is so short. I have to believe in the continuity of life. The heritage of the past and the living of the present produce the future. When one sees the past one always wonders about the future.' I found something very attractive in his philosophy of long solitary walks allowing one to appreciate nature, and the immensity of space, and the great powers of creation. He talked as we walked together. Walking with the step of a young man he said the future belongs to those who get up early. He had collected samples of fossilised bones and he showed me a piece of dinosaur jawbone and the palate of a Jurassic lungfish, and a new type of ammonite that was named after him: Pervinquieria Razafimbelo.

In the marine laboratory I found a metre-long specimen of an unidentified type of coral which looked like a clear glass tube. Eugène said that type of thing would grow in the depths where the coelacanth lurks. He had not seen this monstrous fish, unchanged since prehistory, but a friend said they are occasionally fished up if you let down 300 metres of line offshore in the deeps.

You have to be careful to pull it up very slowly otherwise its swim bladder will explode with the difference in pressure. The phenomenal depths of its home was why it was said to have become extinct millions of years ago.

Some of my research took place on the campus and I stayed at the house of the absent lady head of Palaeontology, but I also had time to enjoy the flavour of Mahajanga, whose name means 'town of flowers'. The broad seafront promenade leads to a massive baobab tree marked with graffiti from the French Expeditionary Force of 1895. Since the early days of seafarers, many Arab traders and Asian merchants have settled here. Excavations show mosques of the twelfth century and a later sultan's palace; a totally different type of influx from the Antaimoro I had visited in Vohipeno on the east coast. Muslims from the nearby Cormores islands had settled here from the time when the Cormores were part of colonial Madagascar, and they once outnumbered the other ethnic groups. While western pirates made a den in one of Mahajanga's northern suburbs in the eighteenth century, and tales of buried treasure still persist.

The strong Arab influences in the city's architecture gave rise to graceful shapes and courtyards hidden behind great carved doors of wood with metal decoration.

In the port there were three or four old two-masted schooners. It would never be modernised because the river had silted the bay and it is too shallow for big craft. Small tugs and outrigger canoes were coming in to unload, one canoe full to the brim with turtles. It gave me the same sad feeling as when I stood on the beach looking inland towards a sand cliff with houses along the top of it. I was watching men in rags collecting sand to sell for building material, mining it out from the base of the cliff, oblivious of the danger to the houses above. Somehow it symbolised the Malagasy's unintentional destruction in order to make a living.

I borrowed a four-wheel drive vehicle with driver and bought provisions for a week, then set out to look for fossils, with the help of a young geology professor called Arivelo.

We headed south on a road along a flattened ridge. The horizon was magnificent for its emptiness. Low hills of harder sandstone were only there because they had not yet eroded away. I was lost for a moment in time and space. The dry ground had little growing on it except sparse bushes and thorn trees. Perhaps the bush is only beautiful to those who love it. But it is where I was born and raised, in West Africa, and I enjoy its vastness.

The road began a steep descent into a lower basin whose side was perhaps the island's ancient shore. As Arivelo explained, spreading out his map, we were in the channel which from about a hundred and sixty million years ago became a giant river and then a coast as Madagascar split away from mainland Kenya and floated south. Unlike the abrupt eastern coast this one was warm and shallow.

'This basin was flooded at various times both by sea and by rivers, and was built up by silt being washed down from the highlands. This level is a sea bed.' And he proved it by telling the driver to stop and walking a short way until he picked up some curled whorl fragments of ammonites that had been up to fifty centimetres in diameter. Jurassic seas were warm and filled with food, and shellfish grew far larger than nowadays.

Next we stopped at a ravine with belemnites sticking out of its crumbly earth. These are long bullet-shaped casts of ancient marine life, a type now extinct. The casts still have uses: if you find a well pointed one and you put your finger on the tip you will be granted a wish. In the past their use was less whimsical. They were used as bullets for rifles, fired by the local people against the French colonial invasion. Arivelo's grandfather had told him he had used them when nothing better was available, and he made the gunpowder out of saltpetre mixed with urine.

We set up our tents among the trees beside a forestry station at Ampijoroa and trekked out from there each day. Arivelo was against camping where we were hunting since the last time he was there he had been intimidated by robbers. They had stolen some of his things but not harmed him.

He wanted to go back to a particular region because he had seen giant bones sticking out of a gulley on a hillside. He wasn't sure exactly where, but had a good nose for direction.

We took our wheels across the Betsiboka River on a ferry of three pontoons joined with planks, bailing bucketfuls of water out of one side pontoon which had a hole. The river was wide and muddy red. Then after driving a few kilometres we continued on foot, arranging to meet the vehicle at five o'clock in time for the last ferry crossing. We headed south-west through the savannah. On his previous field trip Arivelo had reached the region from the south, walking for two days and two nights. 'I was so tired that by the time I found the place I could do nothing but make a mental note and turn back. I knew I'd found an important site, but I had a long hot walk still ahead of me, and, like today, I'd got to reach the river before the last ferry. But I missed it and had to walk all the way home.'

We spent a long day traipsing through the bush under a 35°C sun. The only time we stopped was for a ten-minute snack under a palm tree, and we didn't find the cliff Arivelo was looking for. When we were completely lost we saw a woman to ask for directions but she screamed in terror at the sight of me and ran away. Arivelo said the local women believe that foreigners, like devils, steal people in order to remove parts of them, like hearts and teeth.

The only other person we saw was a man with two spears and four dogs out hunting for wild pig. He was having no success either, but he pointed us in the right direction for our vehicle rendezvous which didn't prevent us getting lost again. The sun was setting, the ferry would soon pack up, we jogged faster, and finally heard distant claxoning of the driver. We ran the last couple of kilometres, jumped in the vehicle and raced to the ferry point, now in total darkness, but the ferryman had kindly waited for us.

Back at camp we ate supper in a dispirited mood, and fell asleep to the rustle of wind in dry leaves. At three a.m. I was woken by lemurs partying and a dog chasing them. Dawn brought a raucous clamour from birds and animals.

All that day and the next we searched the hot dry bushland for the place Arivelo had seen. From one ridge he thought he saw the right valley, so we went there, and found no fossils but a fairyland of sandstone spires in mauve, pink and orange, with miniature castles and towers.

There were ring-tailed mongooses and abundant lemurs in this wonderfully uninhabited region, and islands of trees in round clumps covered in white-leafed creeper. Jujuba bushes offered wild fruit tasting like apricot, and the edible pods on tamarind trees were ripening well. One tamarind standing alone was decorated with ribbons and little offerings in a jamjar at its base. A tree or a rock changes from ordinary to sacred by the reverence and gifts paid to them. The spot is sanctified by the act of sacrifice and, without sacrifice, there is no sacred power to it.

Walking and sometimes talking in his soft serious voice, Arivelo described a local tree, the kumanga, whose perfume kills. 'When it's hot and you go near a kumanga tree, you feel a tingling sensation like electricity, you may fall and, if no one finds you, you can die. When animal or bird bodies are found, they are shrivelled like dried corpses, because the blood has gone dry.'

I enjoyed Arivelo's company, and his blend of traditional belief with that of a twentieth-century Christian geologist. He denied that he believed in the old ways, 'all that ancestor stuff,' then surprised me by announcing, 'Life begins after death. As a scientist not an animal I believe this.'

And as a scientist he believed in the power of sorcery. 'We think that in unfamiliar villages the sorcerers will put a spell on us. When villagers give you food you can get a sickness which has no antidote. That's why I take white clay powder with me wherever I go. It's good against poisons like the alkaloids of various plants; the clay absorbs the alkaloids and passes them safely through your system. So I never travel without it, and have a kilo of it back home.'

Normally on field trips Arivelo lives on half-cooked rice, plain without salt, because it takes longer to digest and stops you feeling hungry. He took his food *fady* very seriously and told me, 'I am *fady* to eat goat and wild pig but I can eat domesticated pig. No head or feet of chicken, no kidneys, and when I drink water it is *fady* to use a communal tin mug, unless I pour the water from it directly into my mouth or from my hand to my mouth.'

I commented on how pervasive *fady* was and how it complicated life. But Arivelo had an answer. 'You can look at the *fady* in a logical way, it permits family lines to recognise each other. Every line has different *fady* of foods banned and actions forbidden on certain days. It's a way of recognising distant relatives.' In some places, he added, it is prohibited to tell people about your *fady*, they are family secrets. I was lucky he didn't feel this applied to him as a scientist.

Many miles south the next day we were again in the right strata for Jurassic fossils. It was easy to imagine this place as a prehistoric swamp, the distant lines of cliffs as the shore, the sandy sediments of its bed layered in colours on the low hills like a living geological map, coloured red, yellow and white in horizontal bands. Arivelo said we must find a strata of white or pale green meeting a creamy type of red. This was the Jurassic floor of 180–100 million years ago.

The process of fossilisation of plants and bones is a phenomenon which happens when they absorb mineral saturated moisture. The minerals can be calcite, iron sulphide, silica or even opal. Over millennia the minerals replace the original moisture in plant or bone and preserve its shape. Properly fossilised or petrified, it has literally turned to stone.

In hills beside a muddy lake covered with waterlilies we found some bits of dinosaur rib, bleached white but heavy as stone, and two purple tinged pieces of rib that fitted together. But they felt lightweight, being poorly preserved and would easily break or crumble to powder. Another site yielded some vertebrae and a metre-long femur bone. Lying undisturbed in place but barely fossilised, it would dissolve into a thousand fragments if touched or moved. It sat in mud that would be washed away in the next rainy season scattering it back finally into dust.

One particularly well-fossilised bone lay incongruously embedded in the cart track, hard as rock and bumped over by all. We left it there. Every explorer's dream is the big find, the great discovery, and I remembered how excited I had felt when I found massive dinosaur bones a few years ago in the Sahara Desert. This time I was more interested in finding out what different types of creature had roamed here.

My favourite discovery was a dinosaur tooth, a pointed one with finely serrated edges like a cutting saw. Perhaps the two jaws ate with scissor action. Sauropods relied on swallowed stones to pulverise their food, and Stegosaurus, the next most abundant plant-eating dinosaur, had a toothless beak with grinding cheek teeth. Armoured Stegosaurus had ridged teeth, not fine serrations.

In Madagascar the most numerous fossil remains are of the forty-metre Bothriospondylus, probably the largest and heaviest of the dinosaurs. It was giraffe-necked and designed to stand by woodlands swinging its head to crop leaves at high and low levels. It could not have kept its head raised for long because its heart could not pump blood that high for more than a few seconds, so it had to keep swaying. With chisel-shaped teeth, it was not the owner of my tooth.

The only other identified remains in Madagascar was a beast like a two-legged bighorn sheep, and Pachycephalosaurus, also called a bone-head for its high-domed skull. Males fought by clashing heads, they had bony knobs around the dome and short spikes projecting upwards from the snout.

It is likely from finds in neighbouring Africa that Madagascar had the carnivorous 'horned lizard', Ceratosaurus, with its horned nose, massive jaws and sharp curved fangs. Sticking out along its backbone was a series of plates. These were not protective as they had a light honeycomb consistency and were probably a device for regulating heat. If he stood sideways to the morning sun the blood coursing through the plates would warm his body and give him energy, like solar panels, while at midday if he aligned to avoid the hot sun striking the plates he could keep cool. A creature that clever doesn't deserve extinction.

Part of what I like about dinosaurs is how they stir the imagination. Evolution went technicolour. Pigment clues suggest some were bright red, yellow and blue; inventions poured out, some had neck ruffs and weird armour; and some had binocular vision. Six hundred types of dinosaur existed. It is still unknown whether they were warm or cold-blooded. If warm they would have had to be very active and needed a lot of food to create energy. Cold-blooded creatures only need as little as half their bodyweight of food a year, but they grow and mature slowly. If a young Bothrio were warm-blooded he would be adult at ten years old, if cold his development could take a hundred years.

If dinosaurs had not become extinct, the mammals, including humans, might never have had their chance to come to dominate, and we would not be here. When I hold a dinosaur vertebra in my hand it makes everything real. They weren't just monsters that lived in books and videos.

The moon was full during our exploration, and one evening by the campfire Arivelo said he was astonished that scientists should go to the moon when they haven't yet discovered Madagascar. Should one not first look at the vast uninhabited tracts we have on earth?

He went on, 'When the moon is full I don't sleep much, I'm possessed by wanting to do so many things in life. When the evening star appears and it is facing a convex moon, I know I can achieve what I set out to do, and when they are together in concave way I can do nothing right.

'I see the moon and I wonder about intelligent lifeforms in space. There are many gods in some religions, others have just one, so I believe equally in God and in extraterrestrials.

'They can help us when we really need something. Sometimes there's a miracle when all hope is past, which sets everything right in a non-scientific way.' Arivelo's spacemen reminded me of the ancestors.

Arivelo said there had been early reptiles and amphibians before the dinosaurs. Most died out but the survivors included the base stock of tortoises and crocodiles, so we continued our search to discover which other monsters had existed here. In an Upper Cretaceous layer we found tiny teeth of small or baby reptiles, ten teeth, all hollow and similar to crocodile teeth today.

Crocodiles have changed little over the past eighty million years. Their structure was a success from the start, the shock of pressure when they snap their jaws is absorbed by the massive low skull; there's a valve to close the throat from the lungs so it can eat and breathe at the same time.

Sticking out from a lump of clay we each found teeth from a larger reptile. The same gulley yielded fragments of shell from a giant tortoise up to two metres long. Two types of shell made us think there were two beasts.

Arivelo had a fine eye for fossils, he picked out even the tiny fossil vertebra of a small freshwater fish and bits of bivalved mollusc, and arc-shaped mussels, now extinct, from the early Tertiary era.

At our camp at Ampijoroa forest station we had good access to tortoises, for this was the site of the breeding farm supported by the Jersey Wildlife Preservation Trust's project to re-establish the world's rarest tortoise. Here I was back among friends. Don Reid, the English technical expert who I'd met several times, showed me some high-domed tortoises the sizes of prize pumpkins. 'Out of the five types of tortoise in Madagascar, four are found nowhere else. This is the rarest type, it's an Angonoka, we call it the Ploughshare because of the prong or gular sticking out in front.' He tickled its dry scaly neck and the tortoise produced what I took to be a look of ecstasy.

The prong is most often used in combat between males in the mating season. At that time the males go looking for fights, not really to draw blood but more as a trial of strength. They aim to push each other over by hooking the ploughshare under the carapace, but they can roll upright again because they have such a round-domed shell. The loser clears off and leaves the girl to the winner.

'At the beginning of our project nothing was known about them, not even what they ate in the wild or how many of them there were. It's been quite a learning curve.

'We think they live over a hundred years. We haven't captured any live ones in the wild, the stock is based on those in illegal captivity that have been confiscated.' He explained how it is illegal for local people to keep them, but there's a strong belief that, if a tortoise is kept with chickens, it prevents poultry disease. Maybe it's true. Perhaps the tortoises clean up after the chickens and keep the place hygienic.

Each female can lay up to seven nests of five eggs per year, which means she spends seven months laying, yet all the eggs hatch at the same time, at the first rains.

Last year the station hatched forty eggs. I remembered back to the first time I'd visited Don Reid here at the start of the project, when he only had one egg and used to bring it indoors at night in case the mongoose or rats killed it. It had hatched while I was there, poking the spike on its nose until it cracked the egg. Now he has bred a total of a hundred.

He also breeds the Radiator Tortoise which isn't rare but is localised. Many are caught in trafficking every year by customs, and a lot are eaten, but they are in no danger of extinction.

Back in Mahajanga my last port of call was at the museum. Behind a screen at the back of the museum was an almost complete skeleton of a dinosaur of an unidentified type. Its six-metre-long backbone was laid out on the floor, though no one knew where many of the other pieces belonged. The big bones were obvious but the chaos of fragments was a major jigsaw puzzle. Importantly, its head was there, about the size of a modern cow's, in three pieces but the nose fitted perfectly on to a bone with a hole for the nasal canal to the throat. I found it intriguing that no one yet knew what beast it was.

The museum was created a year ago by the university, and they would welcome scientific and university expeditions into their region, to work on an inventory of fossils and help uncover the nature of their heritage. The unknown dinosaur was a powerfully beckoning symbol.

17

It brought back a thousand memories to retrace the road I had travelled by stagecoach at the start of my journey. Naivo came hurrying out of his house, his eyes shining with the same pleasure I felt at meeting him again.

The 'turning of the bones' or *famadihana* to which I had been invited months ago was now happening. It was taking place in the hills outside Sabotsy village and as we approached I could hear music. Zebu-carts were parked to one side of some tombs that sat on a low hill among rice paddies. A knot of gaily dressed people thronged in front of one of them. The stairwell to the tomb's massive granite door had already been excavated, the door was open and the crowd was dancing with some rolled mats that would be used to bring the bodies out.

The last time the tomb was opened had been five years earlier. This ceremony takes place every three, five or seven years, depending on the wealth of the family. If ill-luck is persistent they may feel the ancestors need more regular attention. It is mainly the Merina and Betsileo who practise *famadihana*. They say that a man who ignores his obligations is a disgrace and no better than a dog, and unfit to be his father's son, though the cost of the feast and the musical entertainment is often crippling.

Naivo said they would bring out all the bodies, about twenty of them, though he did not know the actual number. Even the Chef de Tombeau had lost count. Relatives began passing the straw mats into the tomb and moments later passing them back along the chain of hands and into the crowd. Each group took possession of their mat-roll, unwrapping it on the ground, and laying out a new white *lamba* beside the remains, then rolling and scooping the old shroud and its contents on to the new *lamba*. The first corpses I saw unwrapped had deteriorated almost to dust, with pieces of bone and threads from previous *lambas*. Bones that had been in red *lambas* (*lamba mena*) were stained with rusty red dye.

The music's tempo increased to a merry jig; people were dancing, a mass of swaying, bobbing straw hats, backed by mimosa bushes in full-scented flower. A man who died in 1982 with a still complete skull was laid out by the hands of his daughters. Beside them were the remains of a child who died in 1984 being reswaddled by its mother. She hugged the bundle in her arms.

No one was allowed to be silent, they had to talk to establish contact, to call in and welcome the ancestors. If the souls are not present the celebration is a waste of time. Six young men were holding a two-metre-long parcel and throwing it gently in the air and catching it with whoops of fun. The drum started a compulsive beat.

Two men held the mat of their brother who died in 1980, and the brother's widow, wearing a beautiful tasselled *lamba*, asked me if I would photograph her with the parcel of her husband. A sad group of children tearfully held their father who had been dead less than a year. Their tears would not please the dead; they knew they should try for a happier mood but for the moment their sorrow was still too great, and perhaps the shock of seeing what was their father, now no more than a bundle of mouldering bits. He made a smaller parcel than his own father who was wrapped in a long shroud.

One group was discussing how to rewrap its grandmother. The parcel should be tied securely with strips of cloth torn off the shroud. They must be torn not cut; they must have knotted joins to break the flow of the power of death, and an uneven number of binding loops to signify that there would always be something remaining of the family property. Even numbers meant that nothing would be left for tomorrow. The inner *lamba* was secured with an odd number of safety pins, each pin being set in by a different person. When wrapping the corpse you should not start at the head and work down because this would push your fortunes down, you must work upwards to increase your prosperity.

To know which body is which, the family remember each one's place in the tomb, and sometimes they put a label inside an urn placed beside the head. People also give presents to the dead, a little rum, tobacco or whatever their favourite tipple had been.

Naivo called me to watch the bones of a man and wife, now long dead, being transferred into one shroud together, reunited in death after many years. It was late afternoon and golden sunshine spilled beneath the low clouds. The parcels that were already rewrapped were being carried in procession round and round the tomb. It was a dramatic scene in the late golden sunlight. The bodies may not go directly back into the tomb because the living may be drawn in the same way, and by circling the tomb that danger is avoided. Also the circling showed the ancestors how well the rice paddies were being tended and how fat the oxen were.

While the majority of bundles were doing their circuit I was invited to go down inside the tomb. The mouth was still active with people moving to and fro with mats and corpses as I went down the steps to the outer chamber, where the air was suddenly cool, and into the inner chamber which was cold and dark, lit only by a candle. My eyes adjusted and I saw the multi-storey bunk system carved deep into the rock with square pigeonhole openings. Moving the candle around showed up the fronts of the holes and the half-moon patterns incised into the stone.

It was quite a squash inside with people crouched on bunks and perched in front of their family pigeonholes. Each bunk belonged to a family unit, with related family lines above and below. There was merry talk and laughter, a mood of collective strength and fellowship, bringing optimism, and renewal of hope for the future. I went back out into the sea of dancing parcel-bearers.

A traffic jam of corpse-bundles grew outside the tomb, queuing to go back in. Many hands fed them down to a group inside who filed them away in their correct pigeonholes.

A tug of war broke out over one of the mats. Naivo explained it's good luck if you tear off a piece and take it home. The Malagasy need a lot of luck. Finally a handful of earth was thrown by various people into the tomb mouth to prevent it from consuming the living, and the great stone door was heaved shut.

For me it closed a stage of my journey; bones recent, bones ancient and prehistoric had led to the renewal of the life force through the dead. After the purifying that follows death, becoming as pure as dry bones, the ancestors were resanctified and joined to eternity. The sense of continuity, which is felt so strongly by the Malagasy, went back to the island's original people, and linked them with the modern nation through the continuance of their land, their rice, their cattle and their beliefs.

Back in Tana I heard encouraging noises on the racing front. The South African investors were real. They had nearly finished getting work done to repair the hole in the racetrack and were building the stables for the hundred horses which were real too. I even discovered that the director of the South African operation was, by coincidence, someone on whose ranch I had stayed all of twenty years ago when I was riding a horse through South Africa. He assured me everything would be completed in time and I felt he would be able to help me find a mount. At last things were looking rosy. While the inevitable bureaucratic delays beset the hundred horses' arrival, I carried on with gallops on Pascal's horses. The wild flowers were changing through spring towards summer and I now knew my way over the hills with their scattered ruined walls and dry moats of fortified homesteads.

There was a mimosa festival at Ambatolampy, near Tana, and events culminated on the final day with the Grand Prix horse races. I saw the posters for this on the eve of the race day and decided to abandon all my carefully laid South African plans. I would take pot luck, go to the races and ride whatever I could borrow. I didn't tell any of my smart friends of my change of plan, doubting they would be interested, and arranged to be collected by a student friend who had a taxi. Dressed in racing cap, boots, white jodhpurs and red shirt, I mingled in the paddock with the milling owners and stable people until I found a man who said I could ride his horse in the next race. As simple as that.

The race steward accepted my entry, one of twelve in that particular race, and gave me the cloth marked No. 7. Then I picked up the saddle and went with a mob of jockeys to the weighing-in room. My weight plus saddle was average at fifty kilos. The jockey I had replaced helped me find my horse in the paddock and saddle it. The owner tied the silks round my racing cap and gave me a leg-up. We began to walk round the paddock while the other jockeys searched for their horses. A field of twelve was too many for my liking, there had been a pile-up of fallers in the previous race. Two horses had bumped into each other and fallen, bringing down three others.

Anxieties whirled in my brain. I had never ridden this mare before. Would she do what I told her? Or should I leave it up to her, since she knew better than I did? At one and a half kilometres the race was to be a long one, and I had never raced that kind of distance before either. The crowd was delighted that a *vazaha* woman was going to compete. They said there had certainly not been such a thing before. Someone rushed off to bet on me before I could forestall such gallantry and tell him to put his money elsewhere.

The crowds parted as we filed out of the paddock in numerical order. No. 7 is not lucky in either Malagasy or Arab lore. The number 6 symbolises regret or repentance; and number 8 stands for war. No. 8 behind me was a wily old jockey with thirty years' experience on a neat grey. Being local stock, all the horses were small, but tough. My mare fought for her head as we turned to run down to the start. I put my bum in the air in the approved manner and held her into a canter. She didn't bolt but pulled like mad and kept tossing her head downwards and trying to unseat me. The starting line was half a kilometre away and by the time we arrived I was exhausted.

The start was a line-up and suddenly we were away, galloping at breakneck speed and tightly bunched towards the first sharp corner in the track. I was well placed in third and on the inside. Dimly I realised there were no rails, just a low bank and ditch to mark the course.

Round the corner and into the straight, the flags of the finishing line fluttered but we still had a full circuit to run. I moved into second place.

The field were tight on our heels, the pace a hell-for-leather gallop, and I was doing brilliantly. Nearly one circuit done, and I was still neck and neck with another horse beside the leader. Now I was level with the leader's shoulder. Should I push for the lead? It wasn't a sensation of flying I felt, it was more the rhythmic kicking, the feel of being launched forward by jet-hard hooves, thrusting the earthen track behind us. Catching the rhythm is essential and, once I had just become part of it, I understood the thrill of racing. I still had to watch out, however, and noticed how tight we were taking a corner, hooves clipping the edge of the gulley that was the only course marker. I moved our line out a little. The mare was annoyed, flicking her ears, but the idea of falling in the ditch didn't appeal to me. The fallers in the last race had tripped over for no apparent reason. We pounded on with a renewed burst of strength. She was proving a gutsy mare.

By the back straight my leg muscles were killing me, I tried to change my grip but dropped a rein, I leaned far forward to grab it and my mare lost concentration and couple of horses pounded past us. I wasn't worried because I thought we could pick up speed and overtake them later; but the moment they moved in front of me I was blinded by the thick gritty dust churning from their hooves. With no goggles, I couldn't see a thing and wanted to close my eyes. Instead I tucked my head further down into the mare's mane.

Chewing dust was horrible, and a glance behind me revealed some loose horses and a group of jockeys coming up to challenge my place. We turned the final corner into the last stretch. Another horse came alongside me, with a young jockey up in pink striped silks. His horse's nostrils were flared and red.

'Go girl, go,' I urged the mare faster and she responded, flinging herself forward and pushing her nose ahead.

The finishing line was a blur in the dust. My body ached in every limb. Thank God it was nearly over. The bunch were now at my heels and the mare kept drawing away until we were clear of them.

We finished fifth out of the twelve who started, though several did not reach the finish. In the agony of my exhaustion I knew I was pleased.

18

The final part of my travels in Madagascar was one that had been on my mind for a long time. It began seven years ago when I met a Malagasy geologist in London who told me he had heard about a forest of petrified trees. He marked a circle on my map, in an area so remote I knew it was up to *vintana*, whether or not I got there. Destiny apart, the logistics were that the roads are impassable for nine months of the year, then open only to four-wheel drive vehicles with extra high clearance. There was one vehicle based in the region, at the Catholic mission in Morafenobe, but no possibility of obtaining any fuel. I braced myself, there would certainly be ox-carts, and my feet. Unfortunately, the area was unstable and reputedly rife with armed bandits.

To reach Morafenobe I flew on the weekly Twin Otter. It was met at the airstrip by the Air Madagascar representative Jerome who said the town *hotely* was unsuitable and took me to stay with his family. He said no tourist had ever come specifically to Morafenobe before.

Morafenobe lies between two parallel ranges with the Falaise de Bongolava to the east and the Bemaraha *tsingy* line of cliffs about ninety kilometres to our west. A small town on a river, it has a Catholic mission, school, basic hospital, gendarmerie and a monthly cattle market.

I couldn't wait to get out into the bush; it was just as well that I was determined since everyone else tried to stop me. Jerome wanted to make me behave like a proper Muslim woman. As a woman I was not allowed to speak to unknown men, so when I said I was going to visit the forester he came along and insisted on doing all my talking for me. He only gave in to my plans for some full-day walks provided I took an escort of four men, for which he volunteered himself, the book-keeper and two baggage assistants from the Air Mad staff. There were no flights due in for several days and he reasoned it was Air Mad's job to provide good service.

So we set off together early next morning with day rucksacks and willing feet. Even as we left town I saw there were chunks of fossilised wood everywhere, crumbled branches underfoot, mingling with stones as cobbles, as doorsills to huts, and used as building material alongside hewn rock.

After a couple of kilometres we reached the first big tree, lying flat and half buried, only noticeable because the footpath went over it. Its length was nearly twenty metres but it was only about seventy centimetres in diameter and it had no bark. My Air Mad companions were unimpressed, they would show me greater trees. And they did, though they were hard to find since no one locally considers the fossil trees of interest.

At the next big tree I paced twenty metres along its trunk before even reaching where its branches began. And for a further twenty metres the branches lay scattered, thick branches leading to thinner twigs like some great dinosaur skeleton. The diameter at base of trunk was a massive one and a half metres. It had gnarled bark and I could see where prehistoric insects had eaten holes in it. Another tree just to the west had no bark left and was broken into many segments, some so smoothly cracked open by the extremes of temperature, they looked as if they had been sawn.

Jurassic lands were greener than the preceding Triassic. Tall forest conifers included relatives of today's giant sequoias, pines and Chile pine (monkey puzzle). Other plentiful trees included ginkgoes and small palm-like cycads. By the late Cretaceous period, seventy million years ago there were oaks, maples and walnuts competing with the still abundant conifers.

The least-changed of these trees is perhaps the ginkgo, its distinctive two-lobed leaves haven't altered for millions of years. The one I planted at my farm in England turns brilliantly yellow in autumn.

We cooked rice to go with tinned corned beef in the shade of a mango tree. As I gulped my first mouthful Jerome stopped me and said, 'You haven't said grace.' Why should a Muslim want to hear grace I wondered and gave them an English version. And why should a Muslim be called Jerome, anyway? After lunch we had a siesta in the sand, with our sunhats over our faces against the flies.

We had to cross the River Manamboha, tricky or disconcerting because of its shifting sands, but the Air Mad team knew the safe route; we waded thigh-deep to an island sandbank, then deeper with sand shivering away under our feet. The far bank was almost worse, being very muddy, and by the time I had climbed it I looked a poor sight.

From there we crossed a grassy area with patches of woodland, palm trees including Travellers' Palms, some cut at their bases to exude palm wine, and we passed the huts of a family cultivating sugar cane, manioc and small plot of rice, hardly enough for their needs. We rose into abrupt hills and in the distance I could see the two parallel ranges, and in the air I could hear parrots calling and the whistling of a hunting bird. Underfoot the grass was littered with chunks of silicified wood, and as we went over a small ridge I found huge pieces of it in almost every gulley; I seemed to be walking on a fallen forest. For the next two hours we scrambled from one gulley to another among trees sticking out at every angle. Circular growth rings showed clearly on some cross-sections, many were complete with bark. The thickness of the bark was up to sixteen centimetres, a great deal thicker than the bark of modern trees.

Seams of quartz ran along cracks in the trunk and crystals coated once-rotten cavities; the hollow heart of one tree was filled with crystals. Other logs glittered with strange minerals that reflected the sun and at further sites I found extraordinary colours – violet and purple, some white, deep yellow or vibrant red, generated by different minerals. Reds and mauves came from iron staining. A group of black shiny stone trees were particularly exciting and were either a phenomenon called fusain, formed by charring of trees in prehistoric forest fires, or were semi-precious jet, which is fossilised conifer.

Wood may become fossilised in various ways, though usually, like bone, it occurs during burial in peat bogs or the muddy floors of seas and lakes. Sometimes the burial was fast as with a lava flow, and often the structure of plants was flattened or compressed in the ground. These seemed to be silicified, a result of absorbing silica-bearing liquids. The speed of the process was from thousands to ten-thousands of years, depending on the supply of silica.

Where the soft sand had been washed out around parts of some trunks, their segments were held aloft on plugs of sandstone. Perhaps the great weight of the trunk made the sandstone beneath it more dense. It certainly looked extraordinary, like an offering to the sky – the art of nature which puts 200-million-year-old sculptures on to pedestals and calls it Endurance.

The shrieking of a hunting bird alarmed us, and my aircrew were ever-mindful of their role as bodyguards. A man with a gun also gave us a fright but luckily he only carried it for defence. Jerome said that apart from the normal type of robbers there used to be thieves who stole women. When I looked disbelieving he assured me his grandmother's sister had been stolen, and he talked about two famous old bandit chiefs here, one who dealt in cattle theft was called Tavuniman, and the other, Talcief, who specialised in capturing beautiful young maidens. Jerome's great-aunt had been one of these and taken to live with his seven wives at his bandit camp. Her family contacted an *ombiasy* who went into a trance and told them to place various things on the roof of her house to call her back. In the end the handsome bandit chief allowed her to escape one night when he was with another wife. She had been absent for thirty-five days.

Our view to the north at this point was dominated by the massive shape of Mount Fonjay. It looked curiously foreboding. An old geologist had told me the mountain contained abnormal magnetic forces in its prehistoric core. The whole region is sedimentary with very ancient volcanic formations. At one place I found I was standing inside the eroded magma chamber of what had once been a volcano. Petrified bubbles of gabbro were caught in mid-extrusion from its petrified crust. It was an extraordinary feeling to be able to stand amid so much frozen destructive power. We looped round to the east, passing an amusing natural phenomenon consisting of dozens of round stone balls, the size of golf or tennis balls, perched on small tees of sandstone, for much the same reason as the petrified wood. The older ones had weathered to become mushrooms of stone. The newer ones looked like a golf practice range. Finally, we waded back across the river near Morafenobe at sunset.

Jerome told me about some nearby tar pits where the ground goes soggy in the heat of the day. 'It feels like walking on sponge,' he said. 'They say there's enough tarmac there to do all the roads in Madagascar.' I asked him if it was ever exploited. 'We used some of it on the hill road to the gendarmerie fifty years ago,' he replied, 'and it is still good. And we use it for waterproofing house roofs and things.'

But he thought nothing of the fossilised wood which he dismissed as 'wild stone'. 'It's just part of the landscape. We only use it in building tombs.' Indeed, it was esteemed for tombs because it never rotted or crumbled.

At the Catholic mission I saw petrified logs used as benches and inside the church it formed a pedestal for the Virgin Mary. At least for Sister Giselle from Quebec, here for twenty years, but with a lifelong passion for geology, the petrified wood had not lost its power to impress.

'It makes me think of the millions of years behind us and the secrets of time and nature to which I have never found an answer,' she told me, adding that once a year she makes a pilgrimage out to a certain petrified tree as a spiritual exercise. I was happy that at least one person shared my fascination.

The sorcerer I met in the palm wine bar in Morafenobe said there was danger in the stone balls of my petrified golf range. As I grew to know the place better I found it full of contradictions: people said they wanted to become developed, but at the same time they didn't want their children to go to school. Educated children tended to leave the area and their parents might never see them again. So teachers very often didn't turn up at the school because they fear sorcery and poison.

On the local doctor's desk was a scattering of pills. 'I don't have bottles to put them in,' he explained. His meagre supply of medicines was mostly for diseases that didn't exist in the region. 'I've got boxes of pills for heart condition, but nothing for our common ailments like malaria or diarrhoea.' Sick people went first to the *ombiasy* and, after visiting various sorcerers without success, only turned up at the hospital as a last resort. Small wonder so many of them tended to die there. In general, he assured me, the healthy climate made for good average adult health, but there was a heavy infant mortality rate and low fertility from venereal disease. Children can also die around two years old with their first serious illness, their poor diet of maize, manioc and bananas giving them little resistance.

The local industry appeared to be cattle rustling. This small and large scale thieving made for few stable villages and children of four were already adept liars. 'What we need,' the doctor said, 'is a sense of social justice. We have to be corrupt because we are paid so little. If we had a decent standard of living we wouldn't need to be corrupt.'

Status in society was generally measured in cattle. If you earn more money you buy more cattle; the concept of putting money in a bank had failed, and the only bank which set up business had closed for lack of customers. Everyone grumbled about the *dahalo* yet when cattle thieves were captured by gendarmes, and thirty were taken prisoner in the last six months, they were allowed to bribe and threaten their way out. Murderers might be sent to prison for a life sentence but since the prisons did not have enough money to feed the prisoners, they had to let them roam loose to find food and, as one might guess, they stole it.

Development in the region was virtually nil. Without a usable road nothing will change. Morafenobe was not an easy place to live in. Jerome kept a vicious dog against thieves, and he warned me on no account to cross the yard at night when it was unchained or I'd be torn to shreds.

'What the youth of this place needs,' he said, 'is a sports centre. We need £1,000 to buy footballs and team T-shirts and to build a football pitch.'

The other side of the story came from the mission. 'Last year we gave them eight footballs but they all got burst because the lads never got round to digging the spiky grasses out of the pitch. All they have to do is dig up the grasses and they can have another football. But they seldom play for more than fifteen minutes before the game falls apart. We had three teams at one stage but when they had other things to do they never turned up for training sessions.'

In Morafenobe football has to compete with a traditional sport which offers far more excitement to a cattle-owning community.

This is *tolon'omby*, a form of bull-fighting which I watched one afternoon. Yipping their excitement and fired up with the local rum, five bare-chested young men in belted *lambas* went into the cattle pen. We all climbed on the stockade fence to get a good view as the lads darted and jinked among the hundred horned zebu surging in anxious circles. The aim was to catch hold of a bull by the horns, or the hump, or the hump and tail and to hold on for as long as possible while it bucked and leapt. As a sport it demands special agility and skill and is practised only by those who live and work in permanent contact with the cattle, if they dare.

A skinny youth launched himself at a brown zebu's hump and latched his arms round it, but the beast leapt forward with a huge buck kicking violently backward and shook him loose. The most impressive technique is that of the matador who excites the bull to charge and then tries to jump head on between the horns, getting his stomach on the zebu's brow and clasping his arms around its neck. The art is to stay there for two or three leaps, then change position for another set of leaps, then slide off, via hump and tail. But this needs much training and precision, and reminded me of the bull-dancing practised in Minoan Crete. There was no taking turns. The lads singled out whichever beasts they preferred and leapt at them when they thought they could see a chance to hold on.

A stocky youngster sidled towards a big black bull with great fat hump, but the bull kept moving into the trampling herd and the youth could not single him out. The crowd roared whenever any of the lads got to grips with a bull and jeered when they fell off too quickly.

A not so young man beside me said, 'Usually you can avoid the horns, but if the bull's quicker than you are, you may be forced to go through them. The easy way is to stay at its side, then leap for the hump. When the zebu jumps you must jump with him. If you don't, you'll fall and be trampled.' He had begun bull-fighting at fourteen. The first time he had been too drunk to feel any fear!

A mean bull suddenly charged from behind one lad. The crowd yelled, the boy side-stepped, latched on to the bull, and rode four spectacular bucks, then let go, pushing off in mid-leap and sailing through the air to land on his feet, to the admiration of all the young women.

There was only one regret which kept turning in my mind and this was that I still had not reached the circle on my map drawn by that geologist seven years ago in London. My theory that it was probably the largest site of petrified wood in the world seemed plausible in view of the marvels I had already seen.

Now I was within 150 kilometres of the site and had pinpointed it on my map, but the spot was unreachable unless I mounted an expedition bringing at least one four-wheel drive vehicle, an armed guard and, the final straw, a charter plane. I sighed and I packed up to return to Tana.

Back in Tana I caught up with my mail and in it there was an offer from a TV film company for me to make a film anywhere I liked in Madagascar. Was there any expedition I particularly wanted to do? I should have had more faith in my *vintana*.

This was my chance. My diary for the two working days before the TV crew's arrival recorded a state of perpetual motion: visits to the bank, to the Ministry of Foreign Affairs for the authorisation; arranging for two Land-Rovers and calculating and buying their fuel; looking for the man I'd arranged to hire a generator from, discovering he had gone missing, so finding another who insisted on accompanying his machine in case it broke down. I was by now aiming to feed nine people for a week, and was delighted to be able to include two friends from earlier in my travels, Jonah the enthusiastic lemur researcher from Ranomafana and Eugène, the philosophical geologist, who was the only one who knew where we were going.

The film crew arrived and we flew in to Morafenobe to meet the vehicles. The stone forest expedition was on the road, though keeping it that way took a lot of sweat and concentration. At the first stream one vehicle cornered too sharply and sank to the axles in mud. Thank goodness we had two vehicles so that one could pull the other out. The winch cable proved too short but we found a towrope and attached it. Hardly had it pulled taut when it broke. So we doubled it and an hour later were back on dry land.

The white vehicle (bad *fady*) often floundered in soft sandy patches as its driver lacked experience. Well, he would be learning now. The Land-Rover was far better suited to the terrain, but its motor kept stalling and would not easily restart due to a weak battery.

At dusk we still had thirty kilometres to go and when dusk turned to night the Land-Rover stalled more frequently. We drove without headlights to save draining the battery and gave thanks for a full moon. But I had been warned that was when the *dahalo* were most active, too. I wasn't nervous but I was responsible for whatever happened. The drivers were willing to keep going until we reached the village of Ankondramena where we were due to spend the night but first we had to get there. At one breakdown we tried to tow-start the Land-Rover on a hill. When this failed, because we couldn't turn round, we had to tow it backwards up the hill. But the tow rope was now very short with all the knots we had made in it and the inevitable happened, the two vehicles crashed backwards into each other. It was about midnight and we were lost. The area was criss-crossed with tracks, some so steep and tricksy that, though you might drive down them, you wouldn't make it back if it was the wrong way. Scouting the roads was pointless in the dark, and dangerous, we had to stay grouped.

The Land-Rover broke down yet again, so we made camp where we stood. Half the men set up Eugène's big tents, while the others found firewood and cooked supper. Water was in short supply so I rationed it: drinking only, no washing. It was three a.m. when I crawled into my tent. The cameraman slept out, ravaged by mosquitoes, but no one would let him in a tent because he snored so much.

From Ankondramena to the fallen forest was a half-day's drive and from there we would continue to Ankavandra, which had been my point of departure by pirogue down the Manambolo River two months earlier.

The saga of vehicles bogging down was continual and we even broke the short winch cable. Since the accident when the vehicles reversed into each other neither of their back doors fastened properly; as we pushed the white one off a termite hummock, the driver accelerated away uphill, the door flew open and luggage came pouring down the road. But I had stopped worrying.

Water had become a greater problem. Someone had poured away the jerrycan of water I'd marked to last for the journey to Ankavandra. It hadn't looked a good colour but could have been filtered for use. We were in for a long dry day with ongoing engine trouble.

At one point we came to a bushfire, about a kilometre wide, but not fast or fierce at that moment, and the road seemed to go into it. The film crew suggested we detoured around it but Justin, the more experienced driver, said it would be yet more impossible to traverse the bush, and the fire could easily spurt up and trap us. He was in favour of following the road into the fire. He won my vote, for the flames looked small, more smoke and smoulder than anything serious. So we crawled on. We did not want to hang about but the track did not allow more than 6 k.p.h. At least such bushfires could no longer harm a silicified forest.

It was midday when we arrived at the site's central hilltop. In every direction lay tree trunks of all lengths, sizes and colours. I wanted to be everywhere at once. The size of the site was overwhelming and from the highest point I could see it stretching towards distant valleys. It had been exposed by the erosion of the whole land surface. What had once been the depths of marshy lakeshore was now high ground; over the millennia perhaps many trunks came downriver to the lake, floating and pushed by the wind or currents to this shore, or perhaps they were a mighty forest that became flooded, so the trees died and fell, some pushed over by iguanodons wading past. What we clambered over was only the uppermost layers of trunks in the inexorable process of becoming exposed and breaking up to roll away downhill. The most extraordinary spot was where five tree trunks were lying haphazardly on top of each other.

I scrambled around in a state of dazed exhilaration, though the sun's heat beat on the rocks and it was a barren inhospitable place without shade or water. In some ways it was disappointing not to see such huge trunks as I had seen before, and the exhausted film director, clearly less than impressed, asked me if I thought the trip had been worthwhile. To me it didn't measure like that. It was a journey that had begun in seed seven years earlier, now hatched. For me to stand touching a tree where a dinosaur scratched its back, was probably the closest I would ever get to eternity.

The final leg of our journey was so bad I realised we had achieved something by reaching the site at all. We had planned to overnight in Ankavandra and meet the charter plane at the airstrip at eight a.m. the next morning. We got so lost again we never did make it to Ankavandra and were benighted once more. Dawn found us searching for the airstrip with a local man as guide through the pathless hills. We had a gendarme perched on the roof who called out he could see a plane's tail fin, so we claxoned hard to let them know we were coming, nearly brushing the gendarme off as we sped under low branches. Not only had the plane waited for us, but the pilot had brought a special treat – a box of fresh croissants to eat with the enormous breakfast the lads cooked while the plane was loading.

The flight took us out over the stone forest and I realised this must certainly be one of the largest sites of petrified trees in the world, just one more of Madagascar's best kept secrets. It is certainly an island like nowhere else. During my four months here things had never been as I expected. Travel had been gloriously unpredictable. I had learnt some of the secrets of the amazing range of plants, wildlife, and other natural phenomena and I had been privileged to share in the magic and mystery of the island's ancient culture. The bones of the past and the seeds of the future were indeed linked through every present moment of life on the island of Madagascar. I had appreciated being part of it and making friends with its people.